THE BATTLES OF THE
SOMME, 1916

Recent Titles in
Bibliographies of Battles and Leaders

THE BATTLES OF THE SOMME, 1916

Historiography and Annotated Bibliography

Compiled by Fred R. van Hartesveldt

Bibliographies of Battles and Leaders, Number 17
Myron J. Smith, Jr., Series Adviser

Greenwood Press
Westport, Connecticut • London

Library of Congress Cataloging-in-Publication Data

Van Hartesveldt, Fred R.
  The battles of the Somme, 1916 : historiography and annotated
bibliography / compiled by Fred R. van Hartesveldt.
      p.   cm.—(Bibliographies of battles and leaders, ISSN
1056–7410 ; no. 17)
  Includes index.
  ISBN 0–313–29386–4 (alk. paper)
  1. Somme, 1st Battle of the, France, 1916—Historiography.
  2. Somme, 1st Battle of the, France, 1916—Bibliography. I. Title.
II. Series.
  D545.S7V36   1996
  016.9404′272—dc20   95–52669

British Library Cataloguing in Publication Data is available.

Library of Congress Catalog Card Number: 95–52669
ISBN: 0–313–29386–4
ISSN: 1056–7410

First published in 1996

Greenwood Press, 88 Post Road West, Westport, CT 06881
An imprint of Greenwood Publishing Group, Inc.

Printed in the United States of America

∞

The paper used in this book complies with the
Permanent Paper Standard issued by the National
Information Standards Organization (Z39.48–1984).

10 9 8 7 6 5 4 3 2

Contents

Acknowledgments

Works such as this have a single name on the title page. To one degree or another that is always a misrepresentation. Many people contributed to this volume and it would unkind not to give credit to at least some of those who did the most. Research was facilitated by the staffs of several libraries, most importantly the Hunt Memorial Library at Fort Valley State College, where Anne Tunnessen coped with very large inter-library loan requests cheerfully and efficiently. A welcome was also found at the Infantry School Library at Fort Benning, which has an excellent military history collection.

A number of individuals also helped. Eugene Rasor, of Emory and Henry College, got me involved in the project. My department chairman, Donnie D. Bellamy, gave freely of institutional and personal support. My friend Franklin Brayman spent many hours talking about World War I with me, providing much expertise especially about the weapons of the conflict. My colleague Benjamin Tate of Macon College read and commented on the manuscript, helping me avoid many potentially embar-rassing errors. My wife, Mary Ann, not only endured, as all wives mentioned on acknowledgment pages seem to do, but also helped in libraries, proofing, and indexing. I married well.

Libraries, colleagues, and friends did all they could to prevent flaws in this book. Where they failed, as they inevitably did, the fault is mine. I should have listened better.

1

Introduction and Historical Background

In the eighty years since World War I, the outpouring of books about the conflict has been prodigious, and it continues. Scholarly conflicts concerning various interpretations of the origins, conduct, and outcomes of the war are also common. Interestingly enough, it is not only scholars who have long-lasting interests in the war. In the 1960s the success of the movie *Lawrence of Arabia* (1962), the twenty-six part B.B.C. series *The Great War* (1964), and the stage and movie versions of *Oh! What a Lovely War* (1963 and 1969) indicated that fifty years had not dimmed public interest. More recently films such as the remake of *All Quiet on the Western Front* (1979) and *Gallipoli* (1981) show continued popular interest. Indeed, Martin Gilbert's *The First World War* (1994) was a selection of general interest book clubs and successfully sold in popular book stores in the United States. Such ongoing interest--scholarly and popular--makes clear the importance of historiographical and bibliographical studies such as this one to sort out the volume of material and provide a summary of the current state of interpretation.

The Somme Offensive, July-November, 1916, is one of the events in the war that has generated much controversy. The Somme proved to be a turning point in the war in several senses. Chronologically the Somme was, roughly, the mid-point, and for the Entente Powers, it marked an increasing shift to British dominance. At the Somme new technologies, especially airplanes and tanks, proved their potential for future combat. Although there is some dispute about its results, many scholars, including Germans, believe that the Somme also saw the transference of the initiative from the Germans to the Entente. Casualties for both sides were enormous (there were almost 20,000 British deaths on July 1, alone), and the British, who planned and conducted the largest part of the struggle, have not yet escaped the sense of devastation--the loss of a generation.

Revisionist scholars [See for instance Nos. 119, 381, 610] argue that despite the terrible losses of the first day, overall the Somme was not unusually bloody by comparison with other major modern battles. Nonetheless, the British sense of virtual apocalypse at the Somme has resulted in an enormous amount of comment from both scholars and participants. The French and Germans, though less driven to the subject, have also written a fair amount about it. Thus the offensive has become a major theme in the literature concerning World War I.

Writings about the Somme are the subject of this book, a volume in the Leaders and Battles series. It has two sections. The first is an essay providing background and information about the situation, identifying major historiographical controversies and the participants in them, and noting topics about which there is some consensus. The controversies include such questions as the quality of British generalship and whether the enormous sacrifices of the attackers were necessary; was technology--especially the tank--properly used; and whether better tactical choices were possible. The second section is an annotated bibliography of works that provide significant information about the Somme. The main criterion for inclusion in the bibliography was a work's contribution to military history, but because many aspects of strategy and, to a lesser degree, tactics and logistics were heavily influenced by politics, some items included are political in focus.

Those using the bibliography should be aware of the following characteristics of the entries. The date given is the original publication of the work. Reprints are indicated by date but concurrent publication in several places is not. The entries are listed in alphabetical order by the author's last name and each is numbered. The numbers are used throughout this essay for reference to varying views and interpretations and as suggestions for further reading.

Historical Background of the Somme

When Europe blundered into war in the summer of 1914, few thought that the conflict would last for years and be determined by a bloody strategy of attrition. The German Schlieffen Plan called for a massive envelopment passing through Belgium and around Paris. This plan was probably too tightly timed to work, especially in the hands of the cautious Helmuth von Moltke. It broke down in the battles of the frontiers and was stopped at the Battle of the Marne. After exhausting the obvious next step--flanking attacks--by reaching the English Channel and Switzerland, the two sides settled down to build trench lines. The Western Front was to remain a stalemate for most of the next four years.

In the East, the situation was different. Initial German victories at Tannenburg and the Masurian Lakes stalled what many had expected to be the Russian steamroller. Thereafter, despite the bravery of common soldiers and occasional temporary successes such as the Brusilov Offensive of 1916, poor leadership and economic backwardness doomed the Tsarist state. The Eastern Front proved the scene of great victory for the Central Powers (most importantly Germany, Austria, and Turkey) culminating in the Treaty of Brest-Litovsk of 1918. Unfortunately for them, the Eastern Front was not decisive. For the Germans and their allies, final victory required success on the Western Front. Many leaders of Britain and France agreed and pressed for the commitment of the bulk of their countries' resources to the struggle in France.

In 1914 and 1915, the Entente (most importantly Britain, France, and Russia) was dominated by France. French territory was occupied by the Germans, the most formidable of the foes, and French forces were carrying the largest burden of combat. Politically, there was little question that driving the invader from the country had to be the main focus of strategy. French command rested in the hands of the imperturbable Joseph "Papa" Joffre, who gave short shrift to efforts such as the Dardanelles invasion to shift the focus of battle away from France. His scheme for 1915 involved massive assaults that would break the German line. The dominance of defensive technology doomed Joffre's plan as it also frustrated German efforts to continue their invasion.

For the British, the situation was not so clear. They had entered the war due to the violation of Belgium's neutrality in August of 1914 and some non-binding agreements with the French. Their long-service professional army was too small to have much effect against the massive citizen armies of the Continental powers. British political leadership hoped that the French and Germans would bleed one another until, perhaps in 1916, a newly constituted British army could intervene and force a peace on British imperial terms. Such a strategy, of course, depended on French continuation of the struggle and that meant enough aid to keep the war going. The initial British Expeditionary Force of four infantry divisions and some not very useful cavalry was unluckily decimated in the initial battles. Taking up its agreed upon position to the left of the French line, it was directly in the path of the German armies seeking to envelop Paris. It played a key part in stopping the Schlieffen Plan's success. Ultimately, of course, numbers told, and the British suffered serious casualties. As the stalemate became established, it also became clearer that the British would have to make more of an effort than some of its leaders had hoped just to prevent a German victory.

The year 1915 saw the British faced with a series of problems. A split over strategy developed. "Easterners," led particularly by David Lloyd George and Winston Churchill, argued that bleeding a generation to death in France was foolish and other fronts should be opened. Their idea was that the Central Powers could be defeated by the destruction of Germany's allies. The most important result of their argument was the Dardanelles invasion, which was supposed to take Constantinople and open supply routes to Russia. The failure of this effort seemed to prove the case of the "Westerners" who had argued from the beginning that the war had to be won by defeating Germany in France.

Before 1916 the British, who were building their forces via their traditional voluntary system, could provide only supportive efforts while the French launched large scale offensives. The most significant British endeavors came at Neuve Chapelle, Festubert, Aubers Ridge, and Loos. Although smaller in scale than the German and French efforts, these battles were similar, for they resulted in little gain for heavy casualties. The commander, Sir John French, blamed the failure on a shortage of artillery and ammunition. Although the future would show that these were not the only problems, they were major difficulties. As word of failure spread in Britain, disillusionment contributed to the establishment of a coalition government with Conservatives being added to the Liberal administration of H.H. Asquith and to the creation of a Ministry of Munitions headed by David Lloyd George. Production increased dramatically. Large new, but still volunteer, armies were raised through the inspiration and organization of Herbert Horatio Kitchener, Secretary of State for War and Britain's most prominent pre-war soldier. More munitions and more men promised better results in 1916.

Entente planning for 1916 was organized at a meeting at Chantilly late in 1915. France remained the dominant partner. Joffre favored coordinated offensives on all fronts to prevent the Central Powers from taking advantage of interior lines and defeating Entente forces in detail. On the Western Front he wanted an attack in Picardy astride the Somme River, which marked the boundary between British and French forces. The new British commander (Sir John French had been relieved due to a combination of failure and political intrigue) Sir Douglas Haig preferred a British effort further north with the Channel ports as the initial goals and laying the basis for flanking the German line as the larger intention. His orders from London, however, stressed cooperation, and so Haig agreed to Joffre's plan, though with some revision.

The Germans, however, forced much more change in the plan than Haig. In February, they launched an attack on the French fortress of Verdun. The German commander Erich von Falkenhayn believed that the French would defend Verdun to the last cartridge for strategic and psychological reasons. His initial aim was to bleed the French army while avoiding heavy losses of his own. He was right about the French defense, but lost sight of his own goal. Crown Prince William, in command of the attacking army, urged greater and greater effort at the price of greatly increasing German casualties. As far as the planned Anglo-French offensive went, the proposed French contribution began to shrink until the French on the British right attacked on July 1 with only five divisions. The offensive became a predominantly British effort. Although ultimately the French would make a major effort at the Somme, suffering perhaps half as many casualties as the British, their memories and histories of 1916 are dominated by Verdun as British memories and histories are by the Somme.

Joffre pressed Haig to advance the date for the attack to draw German forces from Verdun. Haig understood the need, but he was reluctant to act precipitously. He was concerned with training the new (or Kitchener) units that were beginning to cross the Channel. Dependence on the navy and the volunteer tradition meant that Britons had little or no military experience, and so although they had responded enthusiastically to Kitchener's appeals, most had had only a few months training when they arrived in France. Haig was also concerned about logistics: the British had never organized an operation of such magnitude. The attack was finally set for late June and then delayed until July 1 due to poor weather.

The British offensive was to cover an eighteen mile front stretching south from Gommecourt, where elements of the Third Army were to make a diversionary attack, to Maricourt, where the French took over, continuing the front across the Somme River. The main British effort was to be made by the Fourth Army commanded by Sir Henry Rawlinson. The Ancre River divides the battlefield, which is also dotted with villages and woods, many of which became the scenes of savage fighting. Planning was done by Rawlinson and his staff with revisions based on suggestions from Haig.

On July 1, fourteen British divisions attacked. At 7:30 A.M., 100,000 men went over the top, but except at the southern end of the line, where they got support from the heavier concentration of French artillery, they made little progress. Wishful thinking and poor communications resulted in orders for renewed attacks during the day, and by nightfall 19,240 were dead. The first day of the Offensive was a disaster. Anthony Farrar-Hockley in his study of the Somme [No. 207] argues that there was potential for a breakthrough at Montauban which was not followed up, but most students of the attack suggest that penetration on a limited front would have resulted only in the units involved being exposed to flanking fire that would have destroyed them.

After the bloody first day the Offensive became a series of battles with bigger pushes, including a night attack on July 14th and an assault on September 15, when tanks were introduced to combat. The total Offensive lasted one hundred and forty-one days. The series of often bitterly contested battles that made up the Offensive has generated many excellent books. In some cases these involve particular groups such as the Welsh at Mametz [No. 317], the South Africans at Delville Wood [No. 635], and the Australians at Pozières [No. 115]. Other battles saw a mix of units and have been studied for themselves: High Wood [No. 478] and Beaumont Hamel [No. 119] being examples.

A variety of interpretations has been made of the Somme Offensive. For many it represents a pinnacle of incompetence and insensitivity. Criticisms have developed around the writings of Basil Liddell Hart [Nos. 374-79], perhaps the most important early student of the war, who has argued that both strategically and tactically the fighting on the Western Front resulted from mediocre minds covering their lack of inspiration with the blood of the rank and file. The idea that the Somme was a waste of life and effort is vigorously challenged by other scholars, however, most importantly John Terraine [Nos. 603-12]. The Somme, according to the Terraine school, must be considered as part of an overall campaign that built up to final victory in 1918. This school of thought is the modern version of the Westerners' argument from the era of the battle.

There is thus far no consensus between the two extreme interpretations. J.M. Bourne in his recent *Britain and the Great War, 1914-1918* [No. 79] maintains that the Somme was a "pyrrhic victory," with the British winning militarily but losing psychologically due to attitudes provoked by the casualties. Not only does this smack of trying to have it both ways, it also ignores the fact that British soldiers continued to fight, subsequently suffered horrendous loses, and ultimately won the war. Clearly the definitive assessment of the Somme remains to be written.

2

Archival Sources, Official Histories, and Surveys

The are numerous and important archival holdings for the study of the Somme, but German sources are, unfortunately, very limited and scattered. The shortage is largely due to the cost of losing the two world wars, and the destruction of major cities in the second. Some German documents were captured and published by the victors [See Nos. 96 and 633] and are thus available. Most studies--including German ones--of the German effort at the Somme, however, are based on the publications of the Reichsarchiv in Berlin and the Bavarian archives in Munich which are discussed below under Official Histories. Both of these archives do, however, seem to have collections worth consulting. The situation in France and much more so Britain is quite different.

French sources concerning 1916 tend to concentrate on the titanic struggle at Verdun rather than the Somme Offensive, in which French forces played a limited role. However, there are worthwhile military records at the Section historique Armées de Terre, Chateau de Vincennes (just outside of Paris). The French Ministry of Defense publishes a series of guides to the military archives: *Inventaire sommaire des archives de la guerre*. These include a catalog of documentary holdings and a substantial bibliography on all phases of the war.

British archival sources are numerous, though also quite scattered, and much more profitable for the study of the Somme Offensive than those of either of the other participants. The volume entitled *The Two World Wars: A Guide to the Manuscript Collections in the United Kingdom* [No. 441] is a very helpful aid in locating collections. Most of the official records, including War Office Papers and Cabinet Papers, are at the Public Record Office in Kew (just outside London). The P.R.O. also holds the typed version of Sir Douglas Haig's diary and the papers of General John Charteris, Haig's chief of intelligence. Use of material in the P.R.O. can be much facilitated by consulting the *Guide to the Contents of the Public Record Office*, Part II (London: Her Majesty's Stationery Office, 1963). The Imperial War Museum in London also has military records including Fourth Army Papers, but more importantly, it has an enormous collection of personal recollections. A few of these have been published [See Nos. 90 and 464], but the collection remains a very valuable resource of otherwise unavailable personal recollection. Another valuable collection of soldiers' reminiscences has been gathered by Peter Liddle at Leeds University.

There are numerous other major archival collections important for the study of the Somme Offensive in Britain and the countries that were part of her empire during the war. These include the following. (Collections of private papers particularly important for the study of the Somme in these archives are named. Army and other government records are not detailed):

Royal Artillery Institution (Woolwich)
    Anstey Papers

Liddell Hart Centre for Military Archives, King's College, London
    Kiggell [Haig's Chief of Staff] Papers

National Library of Scotland
    Diary and Papers
    Haldane, Aylmer Papers

Australian War Memorial, Canberra

Public Archives of Canada, Ottawa

Churchill College, Cambridge
    Rawlinson Papers

National Army Museum, London
    Rawlinson Papers
    Haldane, Aylmer Papers

Imperial War Museum
    Haldane, Aylmer Papers
Maxse Papers (Some also at West Sussex Record Office, Chichester)

Official histories have been produced by all of the major powers involved in the Somme Offensive. These volumes are all valuable for their very detailed accounts of the battles, but as is usually the case, the efforts of the official historians at interpretation are at best uneven. The German official histories were produced by the Reichsarchiv [Nos. 522-24] and the Bayerischen Kriegsarchiv [No. 49]. The former, *Der Weltkrieg 1914 bis 1918*, is a full history of the war, and although sometimes tendentious, makes up for the sometimes significant shortage of German documents. Also very useful is the Reichsarchiv series *Schlachten des Weltkriegs*. The two volumes concerning the Somme [Nos. 522 and 523] provide quite useful details of

German soldiers in battle. Unlike those of other countries, German official publications also include a large series of unit histories entitled: *Erinnerungschlätter deutscher Regimenter. Auszüge aus den amflichen Kriegstagebüchern. Her ausgeben unter Mitwirkung des Reichsarchivs.* These volumes, often quite short, vary in quality and are not very common in the United States. They do provide otherwise unobtainable details about the combat activity of German units. The series of articles entitled "The Other Side of the Hill" in *The Army Quarterly* [Nos. 488-495] draws heavily from German official sources and they offer an easily accessible, English language summary of the material concerning the Somme. The author of the unsigned articles, G.C. Wynne, also incorporates much of the same material in his *If Germany Attacks in the West* [No. 691].

The French official history, *Les Armées françaises dan la Grande Guerre* [No. 221] is very heavily based on official documents and filled with administrative detail. It is, however, quite pedestrian in style. Almost as detailed, much more gracefully written, and more thoughtful is General Palat's *La Grande guerre sur le front occidental* [No. 497]. Palat's work is generally preferable although the administrative detail in the official history makes it worth consulting when such is needed.

The British official history of the campaign in France [No. 182], written principally by John Edmonds, is more interesting than its counterparts, and has even been the center of some controversy. Edmonds, himself a veteran, often drew on his former colleagues for information and critiques of parts of the official history. He has been accused, by Denis Winter [No. 677] and Basil Liddell Hart [No. 379] among others, of revising sections of the history to protect the reputation of Douglas Haig. It has also been suggested that his casualty figures are skewed to give the impression that the Somme was more successful than some scholars have thought. (The question of casualties is considered more fully below in Chapter 6.) It is undeniable that Edmonds sought opinions from soldiers who served in the war and whose reputations might be affected by the interpretations in the official history. It is less clear, however, that he allowed those comments undue weight in making his analysis. Part of doing history is making decisions about conflicting sources. The British official history is an excellent source of details, many of which could otherwise only be gotten in archives, and if its interpretations must be read with some caution, that is true of all historical scholarship.

Two other official histories deserve particular mention. C.E.W. Bean's work concerning Australia in the war [No. 51] is judicious and accurate. Bean, a correspondent, was often with the Australian units in action and combined firsthand experience with very good scholarship. Australian forces were heavily engaged in some of the Somme battles, especially Pozières, and Bean's account is excellent. The other particularly good official history is Walter Raleigh and H.A. Jones's study of the air war [No. 519]. Raleigh and Jones are good because they avoid the unfortunate tendency to focus studies of the air war on individual heroics, "the knights of the air," and on the machines the heroes flew. As fascinating as such themes are, they do not have much to do with the course of the war, and by giving due attention to the use of the air arm to support action on the ground, especially artillery spotting, Raleigh and Jones put air power in its proper perspective.

Survey narratives describing the course of the war or some large part of it are numerous and are often the introduction and sometimes the only description readers get of the conflict. The trauma of World War I began provoking surveys even before the war ended [See Nos. 95, 239, and 620], an outpouring that continued in the decade following [See Nos. 121, 174, 417, 508, 530]. Other than a tendency to be nationalistic, particularly in the work of Arthur Conan Doyle, these early surveys are mostly descriptive.

Three historians, Basil Liddell Hart [No. 376], C.R.M.F. Cruttwell [No. 149], and Cyril Falls [No. 198] emerged as the first generation of postwar professional historians whose surveys did much more than describe. While each wrote other books about the war, each also wrote an influential survey. Each was a veteran, but only Falls served through most of the war, the other two having been invalided out of combat after short service. Cruttwell and to a much greater degree Liddell Hart are critical of the strategy and tactics of the Western Front. They are inclined to agree with the Easterners that the focus of the Entente's efforts should have been shifted to other theaters. Although his survey, *The Real War,* is only one of a number of works involved, Liddell Hart's writing shaped much of the thought about World War I for nearly thirty years and remains very influential. An expanded version of *The Real War,* originally published in 1930, was issued for a general interest book club in 1970. Some more recent surveys have continued the interpretation that the war was a foolish waste but have not improved significantly on the military history aspects of the earlier volumes. The most important example of this continuation is A.J.P. Taylor's *Illustrated History of World War I* [No. 610], which has not been out of print since if first appeared in 1963. While not as comprehensive, Alan Clark's *The Donkeys* [No. 122] and John Laffin's *British Butchers and Bunglers of World War One* [No. 362] are also strongly critical. There are many other examples [See for instance Nos. 233, 284, 285, 315, 510,].

Cyril Falls is more inclined to grant that the Westerners had a point. Falls' active service extended to the breaking of the stalemate in 1917-18, and he is more willing to regard the bloody limited gains of 1916 as part of an overall strategy resulting in ultimate victory. Recent comprehensive surveys that are inclined to this more moderate view are Martin Gilbert's [No. 245], Trevor Wilson's [No. 674], and J.M. Bourne's [No. 79]. Wilson, whose integration of the homefront with the military situation is excellent, credits the Entente with gaining a small advantage at the Somme, because the strain proved too much for the Germans before it broke the Entente. He also makes clear that neither side understood who had won at the end of the battle or really before the end of the war. His metaphor is the toss of a coin which Haig was lucky enough to call correctly. Gilbert, whose strongest suit is his sense of the experience of the individual soldier, deplores the bloodshed but does not offer much comment about the strategic decision making that produced it. Bourne portrays the Royal Army's generals as competent, but thinks the great bloodshed at the Somme undermined morale reducing what was really a military victory.

The Westerners' view also has its passionate advocates. John Terraine has devoted his career to defending the position of the Westerners in general [Nos. 604-12] and the generalship of Douglas Haig in particular [Nos. 603]. His arguments, which will be further discussed in subsequent chapters, are more sophisticated than his predecessors' but are based on the belief that the war could only be won on the Western Front and once the trench lines were in place frontal attacks against them were the only options. Although no other survey of the war takes the extreme position of Terraine, his views have influenced a number of other scholars [See Nos. 381 and 429 for example].

There are numerous surveys focused particularly on the Somme. In the context of the present work, these deserve special attention. Early examples such as those by John Buchan [No. 92] and Philip Gibbs [No. 239] are journalistic, detailed, and while deploring the bloodshed, filled with patriotic zeal. Many more recent studies of the Somme are very critical of all aspects of the Offensive. Brian Gardner's *The Big Push* [No. 233] denounces Haig for planning for a breakthrough and not breaking off when it did not happen. He thinks poor leadership ran through the British army and that the whole Offensive was of little worth. Other examples of such critical surveys may be found in the volumes by John Harris [No. 285], Alistair Horne [No. 315], and Reginald Pound [No. 510].

Anthony Farrar-Hockley in *The Somme* [No. 207] and Martin Middlebrook in *The First Day on the Somme* [No. 448] show evidence of better research than any of the books just mentioned, and while critical of the planning, recognize that problems of communication and control were often beyond the ability of any officer to fix. Like Falls, they regard the battle in the light of the longer struggle that led to victory and hence as a painful necessity. Lyn MacDonald [No. 406], whose use of oral sources is extraordinary, is even more inclined to argue that the problems of the Somme were the sorts of technical difficulties that could not be prevented by the generals. Peter Liddle, however, takes a very different view, very much like Terraine's. In his *The 1916 Battle of the Somme: A Reappraisal* [No. 381] Liddle insists that the Offensive was the only reasonable strategy. It was intended to wear down the Germans and did so. He acknowledges problems with poor quality artillery shells and criticizes Rawlinson for failing to reinforce success, which cost the attackers their best chance for a significant territorial gain. But on the whole, he regards the Somme as an effectively planned and carried out step in the long and costly drive for victory that culminated in 1918. Although it does not supersede the work of Farrar-Hockley or Middlebrook, Liddle's study must be included in any serious examination of the Somme.

3

Generalship and Strategy

Controversy about what goals the Somme Offensive was intended to achieve began almost before the attack itself. The original plan, which was begun in late 1915, envisaged a joint attack on all fronts--Western, Eastern, and Italian--which would neutralize the German advantage of interior lines and break the stalemate. In the West, the French army was expected to take the major part, but the British, with their newly recruited "Kitchener" armies swelling their numbers in France, were to play a much bigger role than in past efforts. The continuing predominance of the French in the war effort meant that their generals could impose many aspects of the plan. Haig believed that an attack in the north to seize ports on the English Channel and then roll up the German flank was the best idea. This is similar to the effort made by the British in 1917 at Third Ypres (or Passchendaele) with relatively little success.

As Lyn MacDonald [No. 406] has pointed out, however, the German defenses in the North were much less developed in 1916 while those in the Somme area were, as Winston Churchill noted [No. 121], perhaps the best in the world. Martin Middlebrook [No. 448] has suggested that the choice of ground was, in part, political because the French wanted to be certain that the British were pulled into a major and bloody battle after which they would not be attracted by German peace feelers. This was certainly the effect, for after the sacrifice on the Somme ending the war without victory was not politically feasible in Britain.

Planning for the 1916 Entente Offensive had to be significantly modified because of the massive German assault on the fortress of Verdun. On the one hand, Joffre began telling Haig that the French contribution would have to be significantly reduced and on the other that the attack should be large and soon. It became clear that the summer 1916 Entente offensive on the Western Front would be basically a British show. Haig was left to plan an offensive which he had not wanted in either the place or form it was to occur and which the cooperating French general, Ferdinand Foch, did not like either [No. 374]. Foch participated because Joffre had ordered him to do so.

Haig's strategic goals have never been made entirely clear and as he never systematically explained them, have provoked bitter argument and criticism. It has been often noted--particularly by Easterners like Churchill and Lloyd George--that the Somme region offered little or no geographical target that was strategically significant [See for instance Nos. 121, 387, 428]. The geographic difficulties also grew from the ground itself. There was little cover and the attackers would have to advance over rising ground that offered the enemy excellent fields of fire for machine guns and rifles [Nos. 56, 334, 434]. To attack in such a place would seem to require much justification.

Concerning three Entente goals there is consensus. First, the Offensive was certainly expected to relieve the pressure on Verdun. Joffre had begun to hint to Haig that without prompt action by the British, the French might be unable to continue. Seriously concerned about supply and adequate training for the inexperienced British armies, Haig wanted to attack in the early fall, but he agreed to begin in late June (rain forced the date back to July 1) to accommodate the French. The second goal was that Haig hoped to hold German troops in place to prevent their being shifted to Eastern Europe to extend German successes in the Balkans and strike at the Russians. The third of the goals was attrition or in the parlance of the day, "wearing out the enemy." As Falkenhayn had hoped to do at Verdun, Haig wanted to draw the enemy's reserves into play and bleed them until the defensive line could no longer be held. This third goal ultimately became most significant and most controversial.

Haig seems to have dreamed of breakthrough, but he never made clear whether or not this was part of the active plan. His friends insist that he was merely being prepared for the best chance, but his foes insist that he poured lives into the quixotic hope of opening the way for a cavalry charge. Haig did have cavalry units available behind the line [No. 663], and at least John Croft [No. 140] and Frank Maxwell [No. 440], who were both on the scene, believed that opportunities to use them were missed by operational commanders. More typically Graham Hutchinson [No. 323], an officer, and George Coppard [No. 132], a private, view Haig as an unimaginative fool who poured helpless infantrymen into futile attack after futile attack, seeking a breakthrough [Other examples include Nos. 127, 175, 269, 284, 424, 556, 576, 757, 619, 628]. Frederick Maurice, one of Haig's colleagues, called attrition a crude strategy [No. 436]. Such comments from soldiers provide evidence for those who conclude that the flower of an English generation died at the Somme along with the idealism that had previously driven the volunteer tradition of the British military.

Scholarly disparaging of British strategy at the Somme has also been widespread and as indicated in the Introduction (above), remains common in popular presentations about the war. Basil Liddell Hart [Nos. 374-77, 379] has done much to promote this view, but a number of recent, widely read books have supported it. Alan Clark's *The Donkeys* [No. 122] is a vigorous condemnation of the generals, and John Keegan in *The Face of Battle* [No. 345] also condemns the strategy. The title of John Laffin's *British Butchers Bunglers of World War One* [No. 362] leaves little doubt about his concept of Haig's battle. This view is also expressed by A.J.P. Taylor in *The Illustrated History of World War I* [No. 601], which, if the number of copies in circulation is fair measure, has been the most widely read book about World War I. This point-of-view may be summed up by Taylor's remark that the Somme was the "graveyard of the flower of British manhood." Others, among many, who condemn Haig and his strategy include Nigel Jones [No. 340], Gerard De Groot [No. 270], Victor Germains [No. 236], Albert Fyfe [No. 226], and Robert Cowley [No. 137].

One scholar has been even harder on Haig. Denis Winter in *Haig's Command: A Reassessment* [No. 677] asserts that Haig was incompetent and that the planning of the Somme was more his and less influenced by the French than has been suggested by most other writers. The continuation of the attack after the first day was, however due to French urging. Winter takes the position that the British had too little artillery and too little skill at using what they did have to be successful at the Somme. Even if Haig can be excused for not knowing of the problems before July 1, he should have broken off the Offensive after that day. Winter takes criticism of Haig another step by claiming that not only was he a failure as a general, the he also actually conspired to cover the fact by revising his diary after the fact and seeking revisions in the Official History in his own favor. It would be hard to say worse of a soldier than that he was incompetent and dishonorable.

There is another school of thought about the Offensive and Haig. Early biographies of the general by John Charteris [No. 117], Alfred Duff Cooper [No. 131], George Arthur [No. 20], and George Dewar [No. 166] are filled with praise but are more testimonies to friendship and/or admiration than scholarship. There are, however, serious modern scholars who can find little if anything wrong in Haig's conduct of the Somme Offensive. This school of thought is dominated by the work of John Terraine, especially his *Douglas Haig: Educated Soldier* [No. 603] and The Smoke and the Fire [No. 610]. Peter Liddle's *The 1916 Battle of the Somme: A Reappraisal* [No. 381] expresses a similar view as does James Marshall-Cornwall's *Haig as Military Commander* [No. 429], though with some reservation. Although their arguments are more sophisticated, the exponents of this school are essentially defending the position of the Westerners. They believed that once the trench lines were established, there was no means of fighting the war other than wearing down the enemy and breaking his line. Germany was the dominant foe, and she had to be defeated on the Western Front.

The Terraine school also condemns the emphasis on July 1, found particularly in Martin Middlebrook's *The First Day on the Somme* [No. 448] but also in many other works popular and scholarly [See Nos. 55, 278, 290, 598, 677]. They argue that the battles of the Somme were part of a larger campaign that was conducted from 1916 through 1918 and ultimately produced the Entente's victory. They do not deny the awful price paid, but they reject any assertion that Haig was unconcerned about it. These scholars believe that Haig understood that the bloodshed was an unavoidable element in the victory, and they point out that it was not out of line with the experience of other armies. The casualty rate was, as Jeffrey Williams notes [No. 666], a surprise to the people of Britain who were not accustomed to Continental war. Haig was right to fight and should be praised for persevering despite the difficulties. The writers of this school either ignore the possibility that General Haig intended a breakthrough or suggest that he would have been foolish to be unprepared to exploit success if, however unlikely, it came. The horse soldier was the only means of exploitation available in 1916. There are some veterans [No. 548] and even some Germans [No. 275] who agree with this school of thought.

There is, perhaps, a middle ground emerging between the schools of condemnation and adulation. Tim Travers in *The Killing Ground* [No. 624] suggests that there were many factors other than the generals frustrated strategic success at the Somme, a number of these factors beyond the control of the High Command. These include logistical, technological, and personnel problems. The most important difficulty was the inability to communicate quickly between the front line and command to allow modifications of planned operations. Travers does not, however, spare Haig all criticism. He portrays the general as a product of the "old boy" network in the British Army and out of his depth in dealing with the modern battle. He also thinks Haig allowed hope of a breakthrough to cloud his judgement in 1916.

Another milder critic is E.K.G. Sixsmith, who in his biography of Haig [No. 572] suggests that although the general had an excellent sense of strategy he was unable to master the tactics and technology of the early 20th century. This conclusion is similar to that of Philip Warner [No. 649]. In another work [No. 571], Sixsmith also argues that Haig hoped to achieve surprise at the Somme but was dissuaded from his plans by Sir Henry Rawlinson, commander of the attacking army. Anthony Farrar-Hockley also has harsh words for Rawlinson in *The Somme* [207], while largely absolving Haig.

Shifting the focus to Rawlinson raises the issue of tactics. But as Robin Prior and Trevor Wilson have suggested in *Command on the Western Front: The Military Career of Sir Henry Rawlinson* [No. 513] strategic failure may have resulted from the inability to design tactical methods to accomplish the larger goal. A clear objective is vital to any military operation, but that objective must be obtainable by the means available. Prior and Wilson agree with Travers and others that there were many command-control problems that no general in 1916 could resolve, but they also show that Haig and Rawlinson were slow to learn about and adapt to technical changes--especially concerning artillery. Thus the general's failing compounded the difficulties inherent in early 20th century technology.

The numerous studies of the strategy behind the Somme Offensive, then, range from savage condemnation to warm praise. The condemnations positively vibrate with emotion. Often written by those who knew the trenches first hand or from the stories of fathers, their accounts outrage, horrify, and disgust but ultimately fail to convince, as the Easterners of the day failed to convince government and High Command. The positions of the supporters are logical and well argued, but they too ultimately fail to convince. Surely strategy that must be accomplished by repeated assaults of heavily laden young men over fields thickly belted with barbed wire, under murderous artillery fire, against positions effectively defended by machine guns is not the result of good generalship. Perhaps the increasing study of tactics and technology will eventually allow a better understanding of what commanders could and should have known, and thus a clearer understanding of what went wrong and/or right, and why it did so.

4

Tactics

The study of World War I tactics has taken an odd turn--the Germans, who lost, are often regarded as the best tacticians. This impression seems to arise particularly from the excellent work by G.C. Wynne [Nos. 691 and 488-95], and to have been carried into current historiography by scholars such as Bruce Gudmundsson [No. 272], John English [No.187], and T.T. Lupfer [No. 397; See also 41 and 553].

Indeed, until recently the exposition of German tactical schemes has been more thorough and effective than any focused on the British and French. This tendency was exacerbated by the view of many that the Entente generals had no more idea of strategy or tactics than that of marching large numbers of young men across no man's land to die. Studying those tactics was quick and easy.

More recent analyses, however, have begun to look more closely at the approach to combat. Paddy Griffith in *Battle Tactics of the Western Front* [No. 267] argues effectively that the British were the real leaders in tactical innovation. However, they learned slowly and haltingly, and the Somme was a painful lesson. Hubert Johnson's *Breakthrough* [No. 335] while not as complimentary to British tacticians does tend to confirm Griffith's general theme. Although similar conclusions were reached by some earlier commentators, in these recent, analyses, tactics are studied in a comparative manner with attention to all of the major combatants rather than focusing on a single army.

The tactical planning of the Somme Offensive was assigned to General Sir Henry Rawlinson [No. 430], commander of the 4th Army, which would make the attack. Rawlinson was a professional soldier with significant education and experience, but like all British generals in 1916, he had never commanded armies of the size required by World War I. He had little experience with the new technology--especially modern artillery--that had come to dominate the Western Front, and he was decidedly and justifiably uneasy about the level of training of the newly recruited Kitchener Armies that would make up the bulk of the attacking forces. His planning was cautious and sacrificed surprise in favor of a long barrage and a wave formation for a slow steady assault. His approach has been blamed by some scholars [No. 571, 649] for losses and failures of the Offensive, but others tend to blame Haig for imposing changes on him and being unrealistic.

Rawlinson's initial conception of the Somme Offensive was a series of limited steps. Each objective would have careful artillery preparation and then be taken and held against counterattack. Success would be followed by repeating the process. Haig had a grander vision and wanted a deeper penetration into German lines on a broad front. Haig also expected subsequent operations to push further than Rawlinson thought realistic. Although he did not include it in formal planning, Haig may have even have been thinking of a breakthrough that could be exploited by cavalry [No. 576]. As commander-in-chief, Haig's views took precedence, and Rawlinson had little choice but to abandon his "bite and hold" approach.

The two generals also differed about the best approach to artillery preparation for an assault on a wide front. Rawlinson's plans also called for a heavy bombardment lasting for almost a week as preparation for the infantry's attack. Such a barrage would cut wire, destroy defenses, and stupefy defenders. Haig favored a shorter, more intensive barrage with the goal of surprising the Germans and attacking before they could prepare. Rawlinson and his staff had to revise their planned objectives, but fortunately, Rawlinson convinced Haig that the longer bombardment was the best course. In fact, the British lacked the necessary guns for the intense barrage Haig envisaged, and the commander-in-chief's continued insistence that the front be broadened and that the initial objectives be deeper into German held territory meant that the concentration of artillery shells per yard of trench attacked had to be reduced since there were no additional guns available [No. 513].

The final plan for the attack called for a five-day barrage, and then an infantry assault over an eighteen mile front. Rawlinson intended to attack in waves with the barrage being lifted at scheduled intervals, a formation necessary, he believed, due to the inexperience and limited training of his men. A looser formation would result in confusion and dissipate the impact of the attack. These tactics have drawn the fire of numerous critics [See Nos. 52, 226, 285, 340, 362, 376, 571 as examples] due to the enormous number of casualties lost on July 1. Robin Prior and Trevor Wilson's recent, excellent study of Rawlinson [No. 513], however, suggests that his orders, intentionally or not, were loose enough to allow local commanders to shift to other formations if they wished. Such changes had mixed results, indicating that the attack formation was not necessarily the cause of the problems. Paddy Griffith, in his study of World War I tactics [No. 267], goes further arguing that the wave was made up of sections (platoons) which could and did act as infiltrating groups. He regards the British as leading the development of infiltration tactics, although usually the Germans get credit for doing so [No. 272].

Anyone examining the results of the initial attack at the Somme must wonder whether or not there might have been a better way. One source of criticism is the success of the French at the southern end of the front, which J.J.H. Mordacq [No. 456] argues should have been exploited. French units achieved all of their first day goals while only a few British units, those juxtaposed to the French, had any success at all.

The French used infiltration style tactics, but the important factor in their success was their much heavier artillery barrage [No. 1]. The British lacked the guns to provide such a concentration, which was not Rawlinson's fault, but A.F. Beake [No. 52], Tim Travers [Nos. 625-26], and Prior and Wilson argue, he failed to learn about effective artillery techniques and infantry attacks from either the French or the limited British success of 1915. Although there were sporadic improvements [No. 317], future attacks in the Offensive also often lacked adequate artillery preparation. Griffith concurs about the failure to learn, noting that staff reports from both previous British attacks and Verdun were ignored during the planning. It is unfortunate that where Rawlinson's caution might have mitigated the bad effects of his slowness to adapt conditions on the Western Front, Haig's optimism, also based on a failure to understand, forced more adventurous operations that worsened those effects.

For most of the individual soldiers who went over the top on July 1, little if anything went well. The British suffered 57,470 casualties including 19,290 killed, for minimal territorial gains at best. The barrage which officers promised the rank and file would destroy German defenses and kill or daze the defenders accomplished neither [Nos. 127, 131]. Counter-battery fire failed to suppress German artillery [No. 448]. Barbed wire was largely intact, reports of patrols attesting to the fact having been dismissed as products of pre-attack jitters. The barrage lifted too quickly so that the waves of attackers were exposed to unimpeded rifle and machine gun fire [No. 129, 242, 630]. The soldiers were too heavily laden [No. 379, 576, 676]. The standard kit was sixty-six pounds, and almost every man had to carry extra--mortar rounds, mills bombs, Lewis gun drums, barbed wire, and other items. The result was that they were unable to move quickly even when it might save their lives.

The communications system, which ranged from carrier pigeons to 7,000 miles of specially buried telephone wire, broke down almost immediately making adjustment of the bombardment and calls for reinforcement impossible [Nos. 138, 141, 207, 268, 406, 511]. The result was that the small groups of attackers who made it to the German trenches could not report and were cut off by counter-bombardments. The Newfoundland Regiment failed to get word that an attack on the afternoon of July 1 had been cancelled and so attempted to move through a narrow file in its own wire without flanking support. In a show of amazing bravery man after man took his turn despite the fact that the passageway was carefully targeted by the Germans. The unit was virtually wiped out within a few yards of its own trenches [Nos. 35, 100, 109, 138, 248, 473]. Martin Middlebrook also insists that opportunities to make gains, possibly a breakthrough, were squandered by poor communications and failure to reinforce success [No. 448].

Haig and Rawlinson were hardly the first commanders to have to face the failure of a battle plan. The overall Offensive did not have to fail because the first day went badly, even disastrously. To prevent total failure, however, tactical adjustments had to be made so that mistakes were not repeated. Unfortunately, communications problems prevented those not on the battle line from knowing how serious early problems were, and for several days the initial attacks were renewed with little change in tactics. Again there were a few gains. Nonetheless some lessons did seem to be learned [Nos. 88, 317]. Artillery support moved toward a rolling barrage rather than lifting a set number of yards at predetermined times. Objectives were more limited and attacks not so rigidly structured.

A second major assault was planned for July 14. Rawlinson showed both a determination and creativity that had not appeared in planning the initial attack. He proposed a night assault between Bazentin le Petit and Longueval. Haig initially rejected the idea, insisting that even much better trained troops than the British had could not assemble in no man's land in the dark. There would be confusion and noise, resulting in German shelling and disaster. Rawlinson insisted that it could be done, got permission, and scored one of the few major successes of the offensive. The Germans were surprised and almost two miles were gained. This new creativity was not consistently continued, however, and for nearly two months brutal frontal assaults continued. When the South African Brigade attacked Delville Wood on July 15 it numbered 3,152; five days later 780 men answered roll call [No. 635]. Australians also made heroic and costly efforts at Pozières [No. 115]. Fortunately, the losses of the imperial units were not repeated by every unit involved in the continuing Offensive between July 15 and September 15, or the British army would have been unable to continue. The combination of the success of the night assault followed by the reversion to earlier methods does suggest, however, that tactical lessons were not being consistently heeded.

A third major push came on September 15th with the Battle of Flers-Courcelette. The improved use of artillery and other tactical improvements again proved effective, but there was little further infantry or artillery tactical change in 1916. The introduction of tanks, although not very successful (See Chapter 5) does represent a new tactical element. The High Command decided to use the limited number of the new machines available--sixty were shipped from England and forty-nine started into combat on September 15--in small groups against specific objectives. Tanks frightened some Germans, proved useful against barbed wire and machine gun nests, but were mechanically so unreliable as to be of relatively little and certainly no decisive help. There were debates about the virtues of using tanks at all as well as about how they were used, but their appearance does make clear that the British generals continued to seek solutions to the tactical impasse that had developed on the Western Front.

Study of World War I, especially the Entente side, has had too much focus on the commanders and the common soldiers. The failure, until recently, to study the activities of the small and mid-side units and their officers has handicapped understanding of tactics. As noted above, the very good recent books, Prior and Wilson's study of Rawlinson, Griffith's study of tactical doctrine, and Johnson's a study of tactics and technology, have begun to correct this failing. They give the picture of lessons learned in halting fashion and used with equal inconstancy at all levels of command. They give more support to the concept that British generals were "donkeys" than that of Terraine and Liddle which asserts that these generals were correct on the important issues. Unlike those who base their criticisms on the casualty rates, however, the new school considers carefully what the technology available made possible and what the commanders could have realistically known and done. Much study of tactics at the divisional and even battalion level is still needed, but this recent work provides a valuable guide for starting that work and shows a very desirable tendency to analyze tactics at the battlefield level, rather than drawing conclusions from examining the top and/or bottom of the chain of command.

5

Technology

From the mid-19th century on war cannot be studied without serious consideration of industrial technology. For the soldier the battlefield was becoming increasingly lethal. Officers planning operations at all levels had to consider what new weapons could and could not do. Technical improvements and innovations, especially on the defensive side of the line were, central to the course of World War I. This is quite obvious in the Somme Offensive, which was a point in the war when a variety of new technologies were tested with varying success. Major new weapons, some of which would ultimately be decisive, included modern artillery, airplanes, tanks, poison gas, and machine guns.

The machine gun and magazine-fed bolt-action rifle are the popular image of the killing technology of the war, but in reality more casualties were caused by artillery than by any other weapon [Nos. 204, 271]. Artillery used in the war was breach-loading and fired high explosive shells with contact fuses. The expectation was that enemy defenses would be destroyed. With the trenches collapsed, the barbed wire cut, and the surviving defenders stunned, attackers could penetrate with acceptable levels of casualties. What was not understood in 1914 was just how much fire would be needed. The number of guns and shells grew enormously from year to year, more than doubling from Neuve Chapelle in 1915 to the Somme in 1916 to Third Ypres in 1917.

Memoirs and histories of the war have eloquently described the impact of artillery barrages [See Nos. 94, 141, 149, 164, 340, 349, 655 as examples] and deplored the fact that they often did not work. Before 1918, machine gunners and riflemen were usually waiting for attackers, who often found the wire intact. This was certainly the case in most places at the Somme (See Chapter 4 above). For a long time students of the war the argued more about whether or not attacks should have been made rather than studying the artillery problem. Those who condemned the war as the wasting of a generation condemned the decision to attack. The Westerners pointed to the better success of the French with a greater concentration of fire and a significant proportion of faulty shells used by the British at the Somme to suggest that success was just a matter of doing it properly. The proponents of these arguments have been previously discussed in this essay and need not be detailed again.

It should be noted in this context, however, that more detailed analysis of artillery is being done. Scholars such as Bruce Gudmundsson [No. 271], M. Farndale [No. 204], Trevor Wilson, and Robin Prior [No. 513] have begun to examine the technical aspects of artillery and its use. These aspects include sound and flash ranging for better accuracy, the effects of weather on the shell's flight, and the effects of barrel wear on range. Artillerymen knew that a certain percentage of shells would fall into a rectangle around a target. These were "accurate," but they did not necessarily hit the target. The recognition that the army had this sort of information allows scholars such as Paddy Griffith and Hubert Johnson, who are interested in tactics, to trace what could have been known and how quickly it was learned. Thus far the conclusion seems to be that Haig and Rawlinson could have learned faster and made better use of artillery, but J.M. Bourne's assertion of Rawlinson's almost complete ignorance of artillery is unfair [No. 79].

Artillery use improved during the offensive, and did so in part due to cooperation with another, even newer, technology--the airplane. Air observers had already shown their value as artillery spotters and showed even more worth in directing counter-battery fire during the Somme fighting [Nos. 46, 60, 127, 291 443]. Since the Germans had hidden guns waiting for the attack and the weather reduced both flying time and visibility in the week before the attack, German counter fire was very effective on the first day. The initial problems followed by success may explain why some writers [Nos. 448, 406] give British counter-battery fire high praise while others insist that it was quite poor [Nos. 199, and 677]. Subsequent use of air observation certainly indicates that it had become a very effective tool. Efforts to use planes in a more directly offensive manner by bombing--some fifty tons of explosives were dropped during the Offensive--proved its potential but had minimal influence on the Somme attacks.

The British and French held air superiority during the summer of 1916, and, despite the arrival of the new German Albatros fighter and aces such as Boelcke and Richthoffen [Nos. 99, and 653], maintained it during most of the fall. General Ernest von Hoeppner regards the Somme as the nadir of the German air effort [No. 312]. This advantage allowed the Entente to prepare the Offensive with relatively little observation and to use air observers for artillery spotting and other intelligence gathering. Since the Somme is the first real example of a battle combining air and ground arms, it is unfortunate that writing about the Royal Flying Corps and the other air forces often tends to focus on the romantic theme of knights of the air and/or the machines they flew [See for example Nos. 350, 371, 372, 457, 458, 564]. Despite some valuable exceptions such as Walter Raleigh and H.A. Jones [No. 519] and Algernon Insall [No. 328; see also 82, 127, 291], the interrelation of the air and ground effort at the Somme is an area in which more study is needed.

In addition to the airplane, a new battle technology, the tank, made its first-ever appearance in combat at the Battle of Flers-Courcelette on September 15.

Although as John Terraine, Paddy Griffith, and Hubert Johnson correctly point out, tanks had very little impact on the outcome of the Somme or for that matter the war, their use at the Somme has become a point of much controversy. Questions have been raised about whether the tanks were ready technically, if there were enough available, and whether they should have been used in mass or, as they were, in small groups against specific obstacles.

Winston Churchill and David Lloyd George [Nos. 121 and 387] were quick to denounce the decision to use tanks at the Somme. They argue that there were too few machines available and that they were far from adequately refined to perform effectively. In fact only 32 tanks actually drove into no man's land for the September 15th attack, and most were disabled by mechanical breakdown, problems with terrain, or enemy fire without making much contribution to the battle. There was only one dramatic success--at Flers--and one account suggests that this was mostly due to the over enthusiastic reporting of an air observer. Churchill and Lloyd George dismiss the use of the tanks as the desperate effort of Haig to avoid being totally discredited after giving London to think that 1916 would see major progress in the war effort. They insist that the potential for surprise and even the elusive breakthrough was wasted, and use of the weapon should have waited until larger numbers of improved machines were available, six months to a year later.

Since Churchill and Lloyd George were central figures in the Easterner movement and each also had personal reasons for portraying Western Front generals as troglodytic butchers, their remarks must be taken with some caution. However, they get some credible support from Earnest Swinton [No. 597], who was one of the key technical experts in the development of tanks. Swinton agreed that tanks were not ready in either quality or quantity in 1916, said that Haig had acknowledged this to him. Haig also supposedly agreed with Swinton's idea that they should be used in mass, but sent them in small scattered groups as infantry support. Swinton got enormous support from Churchill in the form of Admiralty money for the development of tanks when the army had pretty much abandoned the project, and thus may have been inclined to support his patron. He is not alone, however, among observers, including Tank Corps officers like Hugh Ellis [No. 185] and G. Le Q. Martel [No. 430], who feel that the performance of tanks at the Somme makes clear the mistake of using them [See also Nos. 40, 285, 315, 344] for instance]. Many critics add charges that Haig was uninterested in the new weapon until the last minute and/or did not understand it [Nos. 104, 270, 285].

Tanks and their use, however, have many defenders, also including soldiers who served in the Tank Corps. The most significant is J.F.C. Fuller, who would emerge between the wars as one of the most important figures in the development of tactical doctrine concerning tanks. Fuller [No. 225] and most of the other tank defenders regard the need for a trial of the new technology as vital. There was no testing ground comparable to the Western Front, and that enough was achieved to justify the trial [Nos. 166, 214, 258, 429, 541, 545, 589]. Most agree that Haig was right not to wait to try any possible means to make an advance, no matter how dubious. John Charteris, Haig's chief intelligence officer, argues that the word of the new weapon had already reached the enemy [No. 117], and others insist [No. 106] that the secret could not have been kept long enough to allow final development of tanks without the Germans knowing. Finally, some writers reject the view that Haig was technologically backward and argue that the general had been interested in the potential of the new weapons system for some time [Nos. 252 and 486].

Although tanks did not have much impact on the outcome of the Somme Offensive, their use did show the continuing effort of the British army to find solutions to the problems presented by the Western Front. They also indicate the growing importance of technology in the conduct of war. Perhaps the most judicious evaluation of tanks so far belongs to Robin Prior. In a discussion of Churchill's criticisms of the use of tanks [No. 512], Prior asserts that Haig was right to use them but did so from a combination of misunderstanding of what they could do and false hope that they would produce a dramatic change in the course of the Offensive.

Major technological advances were not the only changes in combat technology that were occurring in 1916. Some smaller new weapons were also tested at the Somme. Bombs (hand grenades), the Stokes trench mortar, and the Lewis Gun (a portable but unwieldy automatic rifle) all showed that they were important improvements and ultimately became elements in the tactics the Entente used to restore some mobility to the battlefield and gain victory in 1918. Developments in weapons technology and their effects are discussed in Shelford Bidwell and Dominick Graham's *Fire-Power* [No. 62].

Poison gas was the one new weapon not used effectively at the Somme. The British army had first attempted a significant gas attack at Loos in 1915. The results were not only disappointing but also destructive, since much of the gas blew back into British lines. C.H. Foulkes, the head of the Special Brigade which handled British gas activities and the key British developer of gas as a weapon, continued to argue forcefully for releasing it from cylinders in front of the trenches and allowing the wind to carry it across no man's land [No. 218]. He was very critical of the decision to use gas as part of the preliminary bombardment rather than just before the assault at the Somme. In fact, front line commanders made some effort to release the gas as early in the barrage as possible for fear that it would disrupt the attack otherwise. In the end gas had little effect at the Somme. Donald Richter's excellent study, *Chemical Soldiers* [No. 533], gives a clear and effective account of the Special Brigade and the problems of gas at the Somme, correcting the exuberant advocacy of Foulkes.

The Somme showed how important the new technical elements in warfare were becoming. It provides a microcosm of the war in which to study these elements as they were emerging and shows how much the British were learning about their use. As Paddy Griffith and Hubert Johnson suggest it was becoming clear by mid 1916 that the British were ahead of the Germans in many ways. They were also becoming more adept at the new war than many of their critics have been willing to admit.

6

Conclusion: Who Won?

Traditional methods of determining the winner of a battle had become less applicable by 1916. Napoleon had won if, at the end of the day, he held the battlefield. After four months of extremely bloody fighting at the Somme, the battlefield remained pretty much as it had been at the beginning. The British and French had gained some space, but it was best measured in yards rather than miles. For many--especially contemporary politicians and later scholars critical of the Western Front strategy--this meant failure, or at best, as Churchill said "victory indistinguishable from defeat."

Success in modern war, however, was increasingly measured by standards other than possession of real property. Ulysses S. Grant understood the change in 1864, when he vowed to "fight it out on this line if it takes all summer." The strategy had become attrition, a word which according to David French [No. 224] developed an increasingly negative connotation due to the Somme. Although Haig and some of the other British and French generals hoped for a breakthrough, as noted above, they also recognized the value of a "wearing out" battle. This shifts the focus to casualties and morale. Although casualties might seem to be clearly measurable, while morale is not, controversy abounds about each.

The goal in a battle of attrition is, of course, to cause significantly more casualties than one suffers. The Germans intended to do so at Verdun, only to allow themselves to be drawn into continuing the attack long after the French had rallied and were using the defensive advantage and to even out the losses. Although they hoped for more territorial gains than they got, the British also intended the Somme to be a major step toward breaking the German army. When judged by the first day, as it often is [See Nos. 55, 278, 290, 448, 598, 677], the Offensive seemed in a fair way of doing just the reverse. Even if the entire four months are considered, as John Terraine strongly urges [No.610], questions remain.

In his *World Crisis* [No. 121], Winston Churchill argues that the British lost more than the Germans, but James Edmonds in the British Official History [No. 182] argues the reverse, insisting that German casualty reports are seriously inaccurate. He increases those reports by thirty percent. M.J. Williams has objected [Nos. 667 and 668] to Edmonds' calculations of casualties, and Robin Prior in his study of the World Crisis finds Churchill's figures defensible. Charles Oman [No. 483], who was employed during the war calculating enemy casualties, however, defends Edmonds and maintains that losses of the two sides were roughly equal. Some German sources also argue that the Entente's losses were significantly greater than the other side's [No. 496]. The dispute about casualties and the Official History forms part of Denis Winter's [No. 677] accusation that that work was manipulated to favor Haig. If in fact British casualties were more than or even close to those of the Germans, the argument of many from Liddell Hart [No. 376] to A.J.P. Taylor [No. 601] that the Somme was a waste seem more credible [See also Nos. 122, 340, 345, 379].

Revisionists, most importantly John Terraine [Nos. 603, 604, 610] and Peter Liddle [No. 381], reject the claims that British casualties were excessive in any sense. They insist that British losses for the overall Offensive, although certainly high, compare favorably with other battles in this and other modern wars. They also reject any suggestion that the Germans got off relatively easy. The latter position is supported by Ian Uys, whose studies [Nos. 635 and 636] of the South Africans at Longueval and Delville Wood are unusual for works in English because he has drawn heavily from German sources. The position that the Germans paid a terrible price at the Somme is also supported by a number of German sources. Both Hermann Koetzle [No. 359], a medical officer, and M. Krämer [No. 360] report their units being devastated. Crown Prince Rupprecht [No. 549] says that at rate of loss suffered during the Somme attacks the Germans could not have continued. The question of casualties is another about which a definitive work remains to be done.

The controversy about casualties is duplicated by the arguments concerning the question of morale as a measure of the Somme's success or failure. Psychological effects are hard to measure in any case and to narrow the evaluation to a single battle or offensive worsens the problem. Furthermore, all armies on the Western Front had morale problems by the end of the next year: the Germans had fallen back to the Hindenburg Line for better defense, the French were faced with open mutiny, and the British were feverishly trying to devise a tactical scheme that would protect reluctant infantry by using tanks. What then was the effect of the Somme on the participants?

The greatest impact was on the British and Germans, for despite the fact that numerous poilus bled at the Somme, the real impact on French morale in 1916 was Verdun. The new Kitchener Armies of the British suffered so much that the long tradition of volunteer forces was abandoned at home, but the troops seem to have come through the struggle without losing their sense of commitment or hope of final victory [No. 121], though some observes disagree [No. 236 and 105]. The critics tend to regard this as a mix of foolish idealism and misguided patriotism.

The German view, although it tends to confirm the assertion that the Entente had the best of the Somme, has certainly been affected by the need to explain ultimate defeat. Erich von Falkenhayn, who was in command until the fall of 1916, dismisses the Somme as having not hurt the Germans militarily, though he thinks Allied propaganda damaged morale in Germany [No. 197]. Paul von Hindenburg and Erich

Ludendorff, who were transferred from the Eastern Front to take command in the West, regard the Somme as a disaster for the German army [Nos. 307 and 395]. How much of this difference of opinion resulted from the politics of changing command cannot be known. Another general brought into the struggle after it started, Max von Gallwitz, calls the Somme "a lost battle" [No. 230]. A volume of German official history [No. 523], even though it asserts that the British lost the larger number of men, regards Germany the loser, and Otto von Moser [No. 461] and Max Bauer [No. 48] consider the Somme the point at which German morale began a permanent decline and the strategic initiative was lost. Gudmund Schnitler [No. 559] expresses the problem in terms of loss of veterans and confidence.

The German analysis, then, tends to support the argument that the Somme was a British victory and supports the revisionist view. The defensiveness of the loser, however, prevents that from being taken as definitive. The failure of the efforts of 1917 to produce any major change in the front, and the exhaustion of both sides after the German offensives of 1918 seem to suggest that neither side was winning until the Americans arrived to provide overwhelming fresh force. The investigation and analysis must continue, although the likelihood of a final or even definitive answer seems small in the near future.

7

Annotated Bibliography

1   Abadie, M. *Flaucourt ou la percée des lignes alleman des au sud de la Somme en juillet 1916.* [Flaucourt: Piercing the German Line South of the Somme in July 1916.] Paris: Berger-Levrault, 1933. Focused on the first colonial corps, which fought south of the River Somme during the offensive. Abadie gives an interesting account from the French perspective and suggests that French success was due to having more artillery than the British.

2   Acland, Peregrine. *All Else Is Folly.* London: Constable, 1929. Much better than average novel based on a Canadian's experiences in the war including service at the Somme.

3   Aitken, Alex. *Courage Past.* Glasgow: Privately Printed, 1971. Memoir of experiences in the war with the Highland Light Infantry. The focus is July 14-15 at High Wood.

4   Aitken, Alexander. *Gallipoli to the Somme: Recollections of a New Zealand Infantryman.* London: Oxford University Press, 1963. Aitken reached the Somme in September, 1916, and fought in a successful attack near Flers on September 25. He was wounded and evacuated on September 27. His account is quite personal.

5   Aitken, Max (Lord Beaverbrook) and Charles G.D. Roberts. *Canada in Flanders: The Official Story of the Canadian Expeditionary Force.* 3 Vols. London: Hodder and Stoughton, 1916-18. Volume 3 by Roberts concerns the Somme. Canadians moved into the line September 1 around Pozières, Courcelette, and Martinpuich and fought successfully, despite many casualties, until late November. There is much detail in this account but not the administrative information usually found in "official" histories.

6   Allen, George H., et al. *The Great War*. 5 Vols. Philadelphia: George Barrie's
       Sons, 1915-21. Despite the limited geographical gain, the authors think the
       battle was justified because it helped relieve Verdun, made possible some
       Russian success, and wore down the Germans.

7   Allinson, Sidney. *The Bantams: The Untold History of World War I*. London:
       Howard Baker, 1981. The Bantams were men under the original minimum
       height requirement for the British Army. They were concentrated in the 35th
       and 40th Divisions and acquitted themselves with distinction at Bazentin
       Ridge (July 15-August 26) and other engagements. The units were later
       unsuccessful and disbanded.

8   Andrews, William L. *Haunting Years: The Commentaries of a War Territorial*.
       London: Hutchinson, 1930. Author saw service with the Black Watch in
       1915 and at the Somme in 1916.

9   Anon. *A Canadian Subaltern: Billy's Letters to His Mother*. London:
       Constable, 1917. Able to write more freely than most due to his rank, this
       author gives a particularly open account of the difficulties faced by the
       Canadians when, in September, their units arrived at the Somme.

10   Anon. *The 5th Battalion The Cameronians* (Scottish Rifles), 1914-1919.
       London: Jackson and Son, 1936. Painful account of a battalion that was
       virtually wiped out at High Wood in July, 1916.

11   Anon. *History of the 8th North Staffords*. Longton, Staffordshire: Hughes and
       Harper, 1921. Although its commander was killed, the unit did quite well at
       La Boisselle in the July attack and at Grandcourt in November. Story told
       effectively.

12   Anon. *History of the 50th Infantry Brigade*. Privately Published, 1919. This
       account is generally accurate and worth reading, though the volume is hard to
       find.

13   Anon. *History of the 1st and 2nd Battalions the North Staffordshire Regiment,
       1914-1923*. Longton, Staffordshire: Hughes and Harber, [1933.] Simple
       descriptive account of the 1st Battalion, which served with the 72nd Brigade,
       24th Division at the Somme.

14   Anon. *The History of the London Rifle Brigade, 1859-1919*. London:
       Constable, 1921. The brigade was with the 56th Division at the Somme and
       took the German trenches across from Gommecourt. It also fought at Les
       Boeufs in October. This is an interesting and informative work.

15   Anon. [Bell, Douglas.] *A Soldier's Diary of the Great War*. London: Faber and
      Gwyer, 1929. The author was commissioned in 1915 and was a junior officer
      during the first month of the Somme offensive and then transferred to the
      R.F.C. He provides a good description of condition of men and trenches
      before and after battle and a sketchy one of combat.

16   Anon. *The 23rd London Regiment, 1978-1919*. London: Times Publishing Co.,
      1936. Includes account of the First Battalion of the regiment in action at
      Ginchy and High Wood during the Somme offensive.

17   Anon. [Dunn, C.J.] ed. *The War the Infantry Knew, 1914-1919: A Chronicle
      of Service in France and Belgium with the Second Battalion His Majesty's
      Twenty-Third Foot, The Royal Welsh Fusiliers*. London: P.S. King, 1938;
      rpt. 1987. Effective account of action with the Royal Welsh Fusiliers in the
      33rd Division. Assembled in diary format by one of the unit's medical
      officers.

18   Anspach, Siegfried, and Erhard Flach. *Das Königlich Sächsische Reserve-
      Infanterie-Regiment Nr. 107*. [The Royal Saxon Reserve Infantry Regiment
      No. 107] Dresden: Wilhelm and Bertha Baensch Stiftung, 1927). German
      unit history with good account of action at Longueval.

19   Arnewood [Cooke, E.D.M.H..] *With the Guns West and East*. Privately Printed,
      1924. These episodic reminiscences include an account of experiences at the
      Somme.

20   Arthur, George. *Lord Haig*. London: Heinemann, 1928. Arthur is a very
      friendly biographer but does provide an account of Haig at Somme.

21   Arthur, John W., and Ion S. Munro. *The 17th Highland Light Infantry*.
      Glasgow: David J. Clarke, 1920. Brief account of the 17th (3rd Glasgow)
      Battalion which was part of the initial, July 1, attack at the Somme.

22   Ashurst, George. *My Bit: A Lancashire Fusilier at War 1914-18*, Edited by
      Richard Holmes. Ramsbury: Crowood Press, 1987. Memoirs including
      account of fighting at Beaumont Hamel on July 1.

23   Ashworth, Tony. *Trench Warfare, 1914-1918: Live and Let Live System*.
      London: Holmes and Meier, 1980. Although Ashworth does not focus
      particularly on the Somme, his discussion of trench war and the tendency of
      soldiers to adopt a tolerance toward less aggressive foes is a very important
      contribution to understanding the Western Front. His book deserves attention
      from anyone seeking to understand the situation.

24   Asprey, Robert D. *The German High Command at War: Hindenburg and Ludendorff Conduct World War I*. New York: William Morrow, 1991. Asprey's focus is more political than military, but he discusses the Somme as a factor in Falkenhayn's fall and the ascension of Hindenburg and Ludendorff.

25   Aston, George. *The Biography of the Late Marshal Foch*. London: Hutchinson, 1929. Although superficial in places, Aston's attention to Foch's relationship with Haig makes this study of some use for understanding Allied planning.

26   Aston, George. "Haig and Foch." *Quarterly Review* (April 1923): 233-57. Vigorous defense of Haig insisting that judgement of his efforts must be tempered by the situation and that in the long-run he was successful.

27   Aston, J., and L.M. Duggan. *The History of the 12th (Bermondsey) Battalion East Surrey Regiment*. London: Union Press, 1936. The East Surrey Regiment was part of the 41st Division which fought briefly at Flers-Courcelette and Transloy Ridges in September and October.

28   Atkinson, C.T. *The Devonshire Regiment, 1914-1918*. London: Simpkin, Marshall, Hamilton, Kent, 1926. Detailed account of the regiment's attacks in July and later in the Mametz, High Wood, Longueval, and Ginchy areas.

29   Atkinson, C.T. *The History of the South Wales Borderers, 1914-1918*. London: Medici Society, 1931. As part of the 29th Division, the unit was in heavy fighting for much of July and again in September. The author provides better context than most unit historians.

30   Atkinson, C.T. *The Queen's Own Royal West Kent Regiment, 1915-1919*. London: Simpkin, Marshall, 1924. Battalions of the regiment fought in a number of battles in the Somme campaign from July through September. Accounts are brief but provide useful details.

31   Atkinson, C.T. *Regimental History of the Royal Hampshire Regiment*. 2 Vols. Glasgow: Robert Maclehose, 1950-52. Regimental battalions saw action at the Somme, particularly at Flers on September 15, where the support of tanks produced success with relatively few casualties. (A third volume of this history, written by D.S. Daniell, appeared in 1955.)

32   Atkinson, C.T. *The Seventh Division, 1914-1918*. London: John Murray, 1927. Elements of the Division fought at Mametz, Bazentin, High Wood, Ginchy, and Beaumont Hamel with little success. It did better at Guillemont and Falfemont Farm, and felt it had been used piecemeal and without rest or it might have done better. More training was also needed.

33   Atteridge, A. Hilliard. *Foch.* London: Skeffington, 1918. The author of this
       study has focused on military issues and Foch's theories of combat. The bulk
       of the book is concerned with World War I, and although quite rare in the
       U.S., it is a useful study for understanding the French attitude about the
       Somme offensive.

34   Atteridge, A. Hilliard. *History of the 17th (Northern) Division.* Glasgow:
       Robert Maclehose, 1929. One brigade of the Division was battered near
       Fricourt in a follow up attack the afternoon of July 1. The rest of the Division
       moved in to the same area and took Fricourt. July 4, it took the Quadrangle
       Trench but suffered heavily and was withdrawn. It did not return to the
       Somme until November. Account is mostly descriptive.

35   Atwater, James D. "Echoes and Voices Summoned from a Half-Hour in Hell."
       Smithsonian 18 (Nov. 1987): 196-200+. Account of the virtual destruction
       of the Newfoundland regiment on July 1. Its casualties ran to 85 percent with
       more than a third of its total force dead.

36   Babington, Anthony. *For the Sake of Example: Capital Courts Martial, 1914-
       1920.* New York: St. Martin's Press, 1983. An interesting study of
       morale--despite the horror of the battle only twenty-four British soldiers were
       executed from July through September, 1916.

37   Badsey, S.D. "Battle of the Somme: British War-Propaganda." *Historical
       Journal of Film Radio, and Television* 3 (1983): 99-115. Describes the
       background to the making of the film "Battle of the Somme" (1916) as a
       function of propaganda.

38   Bailey, O.F. and H.M. Hollier. *"The Kensingtons" 13th London Regiment.* N.P.:
       Regimental Old Comrades' Association, n.d. Although the authors were both
       sergeants, the book fails to provide the N.C.O.'s perspective, but does give
       brief descriptive accounts of the unit's activities at Albert, Ginchy,
       Guillemont, Les Boeufs and Morval.

39   Baker, P.G. *The History of the 1/4th Battalion Duke of Wellington's (West
       Riding) Regiment.* London: N.P., 1920. This regiment was part of the 49th
       Division, which fought at several places from July 1 to late September.

40   Baker-Carr, C.D. *From Chauffeur to Brigadier.* London: Ernest Benn, 1930.
       The author was involved with the development of the Machine Gun Corps and
       then the Tank Corps. He argues that despite problems tanks were successful
       at the Somme, especially in undermining German morale. His views make an
       interesting contrast to critics such as Winston Churchill who insist that tanks
       were unveiled foolishly for minimal gain. The author has an unfortunate

tendency to speak well of himself, however.

41   Balck, William. *Entwicklung der Taktik im Weltkrieg*. Berlin: R. Eisenschmidt, 1922. Translated by H. Bell as *The Development of Tactics, World War*. Fort Leavenworth, KS, 1922. Provides a discussion of tactical experiments during the war.

42   Bamberg, Georg. *Das Königlich Sächsische Reserve- Infanterie-Regiment Nr. 106*. [The Royal Saxon Reserve Infanterie Regiment No. 106.] Dresden: Wilhelm and Bertha Baensch Stiftung, 1925. History of German regiment particularly involved at Longueval.

43   Banks, Arthur. *A Military Atlas of the First World War*. London: Heinemann, 1975; rpt. 1989. Excellent map layout of the Somme campaign.

44   Banks, T.M. and R.A. Chell. *With the 10th Essex in France*. 2nd ed. London: Gay Hancock, 1924; 1st ed., 1921. Describes unit's major actions at the Somme: holding Delville Wood in July and storming Thiepval in September. Casualties were heavy.

45   Baring, Maurice. *Flying Corps Headquarters*, 1914-1918. London: Bell, 1920; rpt. 1968 and 1985. Baring's focus is much more administrative than operational and sometimes he seems more interested in who dined with whom than in the war. Nonetheless he does provide useful background concerning the activities of the R.F.C., which held superiority for most of the period of the Somme offensive.

46   Barker, Ralph. *The Royal Flying Corps in France*. London: Constable, 1994. In his discussion of the Somme, Barker comments on artillery spotting and the problems caused by the weather during key parts of the preliminary bombardment. He also notes the useful effects of bombing. His account is, however, more focused on pilots and machines than the land battle.

47   Barrie, Alexander. War Underground. London: Frederick Muller, 1962. Extensive history of mining efforts on the Western Front, including the Somme campaign. The volume is not, however, well organized.

48   Bauer, Max. *Der grosse Krieg in Feld und Heimat*. [The Great War on the Battlefield and at Home.] Tübingen: Osiandersche Buchhandlung, 1921. Bauer was closely tied to Ludendorff, serving on the operations staff. He discusses the failure of that staff to take adequate notice of the threat on the Somme and asserts that the Germans were "morally beaten" in the battle.

49   Bayerisches Kriegsarchiv. *Die Bayen im Grossen Krieg, 1914-1918*. [The

Bavarians in the Great War, 1914-1918.] Munich: Bayerisches Kriegsarchiv, 1923. Official history of the Bavarian forces in the war which provides accounts of a number of units involved in the defense at the Somme.

50   Bean, C.E.W. *Anzac to Amiens*. Canberra: Australian War Memorial, 1961. Bean was the official Australian historian and provides in this work a shorter but well-written account of Australian forces, including fighting at the Somme, especially at Pozières.

51   Bean, C.E.W., General Editor and Principal Author. *The Official History of Australia in the War of 1914-1918*. 12 Vols. Sydney: Government Printing Office, 1921-43. Vol. 3: The Australian Imperial Forces in France, 1916. Sydney: Angus and Robertson, 1929. Perhaps the best official history. Bean supplies the expected detail with more even handed and astute interpretation than usual in such works.

52   Becke, A.F. "The Coming of the Creeping Barrage." *Journal of the Royal Artillery* 58 (1931-32): 19-42. Unlike the French, the British failed to use creeping barrages on July 1, and although he commented on their value, Rawlinson failed to require them even for the mid-September attacks. Proper use of artillery proved a key to success, and this failure to learn was a serious fault in the general commanding the Forth Army.

53   Becke, A.F. *The Order of Battle of Divisions*. London: His Majesty's Stationery Office, 1935-45. A very useful description of the organization and movement of British units from armies down to brigades.

54   Belford, Walter C. *"Legs-eleven," Being the Story of the 11th Battalion (A.I.F.) in the Great War of 1914-1918*. Perth: Imperial Print Co., 1940. Belford, a veteran, describes the history of his unit, which was engaged at Pozières in late July.

55   Bell, Ernest W. *Soldiers Killed on the First Day of the Somme*. Bolton, Lancashire: Bell, 1977. The question of casualties and whether the tactics used in the attack contributed to the high numbers has been often debated. Bell investigates such issues. Unfortunately his book is quite rare in the U.S.

56   Belloc, Hilaire. "The Obstacle of the Somme Valley." *The Army Quarterly* 1 (Oct., 1920-Jan., 1921): 70-78. Although not focused on the 1916 battle, this article presents the military problems caused by the geography of the area.

57   Bennett, S.C. *The 4th Canadian Mounted Rifles, 1914-1919*. Toronto: Murray Printing Co., 1926. Bennett provides a clear, detailed description of this unit in the Battle of Courcelette, September 15, during which it was part of the

attack on Mouquet Farm and worked with tanks. He also describes its
unsuccessful attack on Regina Trench in October.

58   Berkeley, Reginald, and William Seymour. *The History of the Rifle Brigade in
      the War of 1914-1918*. 2 Vols. London: Rifle Brigade Club, 1927; rpt. 1936.
      The brigade was not involved until August and September but then its
      battalions fought at Delville Wood, Guillemont and Flers-Courcelette and
      later at Morval and Transloy Ridges and the Ancre. This is a solid account of
      the action.

59   Bewsher, F.W. *The History of the 51st (Highland) Division*. Edinburgh:
      William Blackwood and Sons, 1921. Well-written account of the Division's
      actions, most importantly an attack on Beaumont Hamel.

60   Bickers, Richard Townshend. *The First Great Air War*. London: Hodder and
      Stoughton, 1988. Bickers does a good job of presenting the air battle at the
      Somme as part of the offensive and discussing the R.F.C.'s efforts at infantry
      support.

61   Bidou, Henry. *Histoire de la Grande Guerre*. [History of the Great War.] Paris:
      Gallimard, 1936. Solid survey of the war which, despite the limited French
      participation, devotes a chapter to the Somme.

62   Bidwell, Shelford, and Dominick Graham. *Fire-Power: British Army Weapons
      and Theories of War 1904-45*. London: Allen and Unwin, 1982. These
      authors provide an informative discussion of weaponry available for the
      Somme offensive including the new Lewis Gun and the improved grenade or
      Mills Bomb.

63   Bill, C.A. *The 15th Battalion Royal Warwickshire Regiment in the Great War*.
      Birmingham: Cornish Brothers, 1932. Provides an effective account of the
      unit in combat in the area of High Wood and Angle Wood near Montauban in
      July, 1916.

64   Bishop, William Avery. *Winged Warfare*. London: Hodder and Stoughton,
      1918; rpt. 1967 and 1976. Bishop provides an account of his service with 60
      Squadron which provided a major part of the British air effort, winning and
      holding air superiority at the Somme.

65   Blake, Robert, ed. *The Private Papers of Douglas Haig, 1914-1919*. London:
      Eyre and Spottiswoode, 1952. Haig was British commander-in-chief on the
      Western Front, and Blake's collection of his papers provides insight into his
      thinking about strategy and preparation for the Battle of the Somme. This
      volume is better than most collections of private papers, but relies entirely on

the typed version of Haig's diary which, when compared to the handwritten version, shows revision in the author's favor.

66   Blaker, Richard. *Medal Without Bar*. London: Hodder and Stoughton, 1930. Blaker has written a very realistic novel from the point-of-view of an artilleryman, and in addition to portraying the conditions of the soldier, has given an excellent overview of the mechanics of artillery.

67   Blunden, Edmund. *Undertones of War*. London: Cobden-Sanderson, 1928; rpt. 1978. A classic account of the experience of war in the trenches by a poet who served with the 11th Royal Sussex.

68   Bond, Brian, ed. *The First World War and British Military History*. Oxford: Clarendon Press, 1991. The essays in this volume are essential to any historiographical study of World War I. Most of the controversies concerning interpretations of the Somme are addressed.

69   Bond, Brian, and Simon Robbins, eds. *Staff Officer: The Diaries of Walter Guiness (First Lord Moyne) 1914-1918*. London: Leo Cooper, 1987. Choppy and personal account of an officer with the 11th Cheshires from late August to the end of the Somme campaign.

70   Bond, R.C. *King's Own Yorkshire Light Infantry in the Great War, 1914-1918*. London: Percy Lund, Humphries, 1930. Well-written account of numerous actions at the Somme, but the author is overwhelmed by detail at times.

71   Bone, Muirhead. *The Western Front*. 2 Vols. London: Country Life, 1917. Bone's excellent drawings provide a visual reference for the battlefields of the war including the Somme.

72   Boraston, J.H., ed. *Sir Douglas Haig's Despatches 1914-18* London and Toronto: Dent, 1919; rpt. 1979. This is a collection of Haig's reports to the government written every six months during his command. They are, in some senses, political documents. The editor, an associate and admirer of Haig, offers no comment or analysis.

73   Boraston, J.H., and E.O. Bax. *The Eighth Division in the War, 1914-1918*. London: Medici Society, 1926. The Division was badly battered on July 1st when it attacked near Ovillers. In October and November, it returned to the Somme to help in the assault on the Transloy line. This account of the Division's activity is good, but the authors seem too eager to praise Haig and assert overall success for the offensive.

74   Bordeaux, Henry. "De la Maison Natale de Foch au Tombeau des Invalides."

[Foch: From Birthplace to Tomb.] *Ecrits de Paris* 167 (1958): 67-73. Biographical sketch of Foch including evaluation of his tactics at the Somme.

75   Bordeaux, Henry. *General Maistre*. Paris: Crès, 1924. Although not a good biography, this book concerns the commander of the French XXI Corps which was at the Somme from August, 1916 to January, 1917, and so it is useful for information about the French contribution to the battles.

76   Bordeaux, Henry. *Georges Guynemer: Knight of the Air*. New Haven: Yale University Press, 1918; rpt. 1972. Guynemer was heavily involved in the successful allied air effort at the Somme. Unfortunately, following the flyer's own letters, his biographer focuses on single combat with German flyers rather than telling the larger story of the offensive.

77   Bott, A.J. *An Airman's Outing*. Toronto: McClelland, Goodchild and Steward, 1917; rpt. 1986. Very chatty and anecdotal account by a pilot who served over the Somme.

78   Bourget, J.M. *Les Origines de la Victoire: Histoire raisonée de la guerre mondiale*. [The Origins of Victory: Analytical History of the World War.] Paris: Renaissance du Livre, 1924. Effective discussion of the war from the French point-of-view. The author's conclusion about the Somme is that it proved that courage was useless against machine guns.

79   Bourne, J.M. *Britain and the Great War 1914-1918*. London: Edward Arnold, 1989. An excellent and balanced survey covering both military and domestic aspects of the war. The author seems inclined to the revisionist view that the Somme represented part of a larger campaign and as such was a success, but he sometimes over qualifies his views.

80   Boustead, Hugh. *The Wind of Morning: The Autobiography of Hugh Boustead*. London: Chatto and Windus, 1971. Boustead offers a brief but vivid account of the South Africans (he was with the South African Scottish) at Delville Wood.

81   Bowyer, Chaz. *Albert Ball*. London: William Kimber, 1977. Well-written biography of the English ace who had a share in winning and holding air superiority over the Somme.

82   Boyle, Andrew. *Trenchard*. London: Collins, 1962. Provides information about planning and implementation of air power at the Somme.

83   Bray, A.T. *The Battle of the Somme, 1916: A Bibliography*. Ann Arbor: University Microfilms, 1967. Originally a thesis for a librarian's degree in

Britain, this work is dated and overly focused on holdings in British libraries. It does, however, note some obscure sources (no annotations) and is strong concerning tanks.

84   Bréant, Commandant. *De L'Alsace à la Somme: Souvenirs du Front.* [From Alsace to the Somme: Recollections of the Front.] Paris: Librairie Hachette, 1917. Bréant provides a full chapter of observations of the Somme, a relatively rare French view.

85   Brennfleck, Joseph K. *Das Königlich Bayerische 16 Infanterie-Regiment Grossherzog Ferinand von Toskana.* [The Royal 16th Bavarian (Duke Ferdinand von Toskana's) Infantry Regiment.] Munich: Bayerisches Kriegs-archiv, 1931. Effective unit history including discussion of defense at Longueval.

86   Brett, G.A. *A History of the 2nd Battalion the Monmouthshire Regiment.* Pontypool: Hughes and Son, The Griffin Press, 1933. This was a pioneer unit assigned to the 29th Division at the Somme. The account of its activity gives a useful picture of logistics in the battle.

87   Briscoe, Walter A. and H. Russell Stannard. *Captain Ball, V.C.* London: Jenkins, 1918. Superficial biography of the great English flying ace who won renown over the Somme.

88   Brooke, A.F. "The Evolution of Artillery in the Great War." *Journal of the Royal Artillery* 51 (1924-25): 359-72; 52 (1925-26): 37-51, 369-87. Artillery proved to be the most effective and dominant weaponry on the Western Front. The development of the technology and tactics, although not fully appreciated by high command in time for the Somme, was a key to the outcome of the war.

89   Brown, Malcolm. *Tommy Goes to War.* London: Dent, 1978. Well illustrated portrayal of the experience of the typical British soldier, including significant comment about the Somme.

90   Brown, Malcolm, ed. *The Imperial War Museum Book of the First World War: A Great Conflict Recalled in Previously Unpublished Letters, Diaries, and Memoirs.* London: Sidgwick and Jackson, 1991. Drawing from the large collection held by the Imperial War Museum, Brown provides a number of short first-hand accounts of action at the Somme.

91   Browne, D. G. *The Tank in Action.* Edinburgh: William Blackwood and Sons, 1920. In his chapter concerning the Somme the author rejects detailed description because tactics were of necessity experimental and records not

very complete. He notes problems of terrain and training and asserts that despite individual successes there was general failure. He comments on the exaggerated disdain of the press, which he obviously does not care for, and indicates that the need for technical improvements was clear. He does not make much general comment about the wisdom of use.

92 Buchan, John. *The Battle of the Somme*. London: Thomas Nelson and Sons, 1916. Book is a compilation of the articles Buchan wrote day to day while covering the battle. The lengthy account, constrained by wartime controls, is not always accurate. Published in numerous versions.

93 Buchan, John. *History of the Royal Scots Fusiliers, 1678-1918*. London: Thomas Nelson, 1920. The author has attempted to cover too much in this volume, and the events of World War I are crowded in at the end. Buchan is a competent historian, however, and does manage an overview of the actions of the Royal Scots Fusiliers in the war.

94 Buchan, John. *The History of the South African Forces in France*. London: Thomas Nelson and Sons, 1920; rpt. 1992. Has a chapter about the bitter struggle at Delville Wood which the South Africans held for five days under heavy shelling and counter-attacks. Much of the wood was eventually lost. A second chapter describes fighting at Butte de Warlencourt in October.

95 Buchan, John. *Nelson's History of the War*. 24 Vols. London: Thomas Nelson, 1915-19; also published in 4 Vols. as History of the Great War (1921-22). Volume 16 of the 24 is devoted to the Somme. Written in haste by a correspondent who was later Director of Information, this work has many errors. The 4 volume version is revised but still less than trustworthy.

96 Bülow, Karl Paul Wilhelm von. *Experience of the German 1st Army in the Somme Battle*. Washington, D.C.: Press of the Engineer School, 1917. Bülow's report, captured and translated by the British, was published as a U.S. government document. The German general gives a detailed description of the German defense and credits the British with good tactics, except that their officers were not well trained. He credits the German failure particularly to the inability to counter allied air superiority and artillery (despite the large number of duds) and the decision not to use defense in depth.

97 Burrows, A.R. *The 1st Battalion the Faugh-a-Ballaghs in the Great War*. Aldershot: Gale and Polden, 1925. Excellent history of 1st Battalion the Royal Irish Fusiliers who were supposed to be in second attack on July 1st but were not committed. The Battalion was not in combat until failed attack at Le Transloy on October 12. Remained in line until December.

98   Burrows, John W. *The Essex Regiment*. 6 Vols. Southend-on-Sea: John H.
      Burrows and Sons, [1923-35.] Volumes cover the regiment's activity
      battalion by battalion, including descriptions of fighting at various places on
      the Somme.

99   Burrows, William E. *Richthofen: A True History of the Red Baron*. New York:
      Harcourt, Brace and World, 1969. Richthofen, early in his career, arrived at
      the Somme in the fall. He became part of the German effort to regain parity
      in the air.

100   Burton, O.E. *The Silent Division: New Zealanders at the Front, 1914-1919*.
      Sydney: Angus and Robertson, 1935. The book is a memoir. Unit arrived
      at Somme September 9 and made attack on the Flers Trench on the 15th. Had
      two tanks to help, but English units failed and so did the attack. New
      Zealanders remained in the area until early October. Author is obviously very
      proud of his countrymen's efforts and bitter about the price they paid.

101   Butler, A. G., R.M. Downes, F.A. Maguire, and R.W. Cilento, *The Australian
      Army Medical Services in the War of 1914-1918*. 3 Vols. Melbourne:
      Australian War Memorial, 1930-43. Part of the official history of the
      Australian forces, this volume traces the medical corps from its origins,
      briefly, becoming much more detailed with the World War I campaigns. It
      has the usual official history detail.

102   Buxton, Andrew. *The Rifle Brigade: A Memoir*. Edited by Edward S. Woods.
      London: Robert Scott, 1918. A very personal account of the battle of
      Guillemont (August 18-22) with little context.

103   Cable, Boyd. *Grapes of Wrath*. London: Smith, Elder, 1917. Cable's novel is
      based on the Somme, but he asserts that it is intended to present an account
      of what a major offensive was like for the average soldier and is not a history.

104   Cameron, James. *1916--Year of Decision*. London: Oldbourne, 1962. Popular
      history more focused on politics than war, but giving the Somme due
      attention. Cameron is critical of Haig, asserting that the general rose more
      due to social influence than merit. He argues that Haig wasted lives and the
      surprise value of the tank at the Somme, though he does acknowledge that
      Ludendorff admitted that the battle wore down the Germans.

105   Carrington, C.E. "Kitchener's Army: The Somme and After." *Journal of the
      Royal United Services Institute for Defense Studies* 123 (1978): 15-20.
      Carrington maintains that before the Somme there was a sense of idealistic
      crusading among the soldiers, but after the offensive, the idealism declined
      notably.

106   Carrington, Charles E. *Soldier from the Wars Returning*. London: Hutchinson, 1965. This volume was written after World War II, in which the author was a staff officer. He defends Haig and the other generals as being as good as any available. He maintains that tanks would have done better with more development, but does not believe the secret could have been kept, so using them at the Somme did not waste the surprise factor.

107   Cartier, Raymond et Jean-Pierre. *La première Guerre Mondiale*. [The First World War.] 2 Vols. Paris: Presses de la Cité, 1982-84. The discussion of the Somme is in volume two, and although attention is given to the relationship between Haig and Joffre, the discussion of the offensive is brief.

108   Cary, A.D.L., Stouppe McCance, and C.H. Dudley Ward. *Regimental Records of the Royal Welsh Fusiliers*. 4 Vols. London: Foster Groom, 1921-29. History of the regiment from its origins. Very detailed account of activities at the Somme: July 1-13 at Battle of Albert attacking the Quadrilateral. Later fought at Guillemont, Delville Wood, High Wood, Morval, Transloy Ridge, and the Ancre.

109   Cave, Joy B. *What Became of Corporal Pittman?* Portugal Cove, Newfoundland: Breakwater Books, 1976. This portrayal of the Royal Newfoundland Regiment, which was virtually wiped out at the Somme, is particularly effective at setting the unit's tragedy in the context of its homeland.

110   Chalmers, Thomas, compiler. *The History of the 15th Battalion*. Glasgow: John McCallum, 1934. This unit was attached to the 97th Brigade, 32nd Division during the Somme campaign. It saw action during the first two weeks of July and again in October and November.

111   Chalmers, Thomas, ed. *A Saga of Scotland: History of the 16th Battalion, The Highland Light Infantry*. Glasgow: John McCallum, [1930.] The 16th (2nd Glasgow) Battalion saw action at the Battle of the Ancre in November, 1916.

112   Chapman, Guy. *A Passionate Prodigality: Fragments of Autobiography*. London: Nicholson and Watson, 1933; rpt. 1966. Very personal and impressionistic review of what the battle and the war meant to soldiers.

113   Chapman, Guy, ed. *Vain Glory: A Miscellany of the Great War*. London: Cassell, 1937; 2nd ed. 1968. Powerfully evokes the horrors of combat in the words of the soldiers, but provides little context. Chapter on the Somme is quite good.

114   Charbonneau, Jean. *Études tactiques sur de la Grande Guerre. Operations du*

1er Corps Colonial [Tactical Studies of the Grand War: Operations of the 1st Colonial Corps.] Paris: Charles-Lavauzelle, 1926. Charbonneau looks at three actions involving the colonial corps in this excellent history. The first is its participation in breaking the German line on the British right in the initial attack at the Somme. He argues that the most important lessons learned involved the deployment of infantry and use of combined arms.

115 Charlton, Peter. *Pozières 1916: Australians on the Somme.* London: Leo Cooper in association with Secker and Warburg, 1986. An excellent description of the Australians in action at Pozières in mid-July and well balanced to give due credit to English as well as Australian units. One of the best descriptions of a battle in the Somme offensive.

116 Charteris, John. *At G.H.Q.* London: Cassell, 1931. Charteris was Haig's chief intelligence officer, and wrote his book from notes kept day to day with memories added as available and needed. Germans could not have taken another Somme, he says. Gives daily (with some gaps) account of activities at H.Q., though he ignores or does not know of some controversies--Rawlinson's night attack called brilliant with no reference to disputes about the idea. Many "frockcoats" visit and he gives H.Q.'s views of each.

117 Charteris, John. *Field-Marshal Earl Haig.* London: Cassell, 1929. The author was an associate and admirer of Haig, and suggests that the goals of the Somme were helping relieve pressure on Verdun and wearing down the German army. He believed that the Germans already had hints of tanks, and so the decision to use them made sense. And they were of material assistance. Cites Ludendorff's memoirs to the effect that 1916 exhausted the Germans on the Western Front.

118 Chasseaud, Peter. *Topography of Armageddon.* London: Mapbooks, 1991. Provides trench maps of the British army front plus comments about the influence of topography.

119 Cheyne, G.Y. *The Last Great Battle of the Somme: Beaumont Hamel, 1916.* Edinburgh: John Donald, 1988. Much of the book is background concerning the British army and its equipment, but the author is of the school that argues that the Somme was the key turning point in the war.

120 Christienne, Charles, et al. *Histoire de Aviation Militaire Française.* [History of French Military Aviation.] Paris: Charles Lavauzelle, 1980. Provides a good picture of French bombing of communications and logistics at the Somme.

121 Churchill, Winston S. *The World Crisis*, 5 Vols. London: Thornton Butter-
     worth, 1923-29; numerous rpts. Churchill's excellent prose would make these
     volumes worth reading even if they were not important intellectually. They
     are packed with inside information especially, for the period when the author
     was in the government, and offer a powerful defense of his preference for
     shifting the main military effort away from the Western Front. He is quite
     critical of the Somme, insisting that the flower of a generation was wasted for
     little gain and that the potential surprise of tanks was also squandered in a
     vain attempt to make disaster seem like success.

122 Clark, Alan. *The Donkeys*. London: Hutchinson, 1961. Although focused on
     1915, this volume establishes the case for poor English generalship, noting
     many mistakes that were repeated on the Somme. It also highlights the
     political intrigues that marked the struggles of the English high command as
     generals struggled to secure advancement for themselves and their proteges.
     Critics have questioned the depth of Clark's scholarship.

123 Cole, Christopher. *Royal Flying Corps, 1915-16*. London: William Kimber,
     1969. Cole provides a solid account of the R.F.C., which controlled the air
     during the Somme offensive and provided very valuable spotting for the
     artillery.

124 Colin, H. *La Division de Fer 1914-1918*. [The Iron Division, 1914-1918.]
     Paris: Payot, 1930. The title reference is to the 11th Division of XX Corps,
     Foch's original command, which was positioned next to the British at the
     Somme. The book provides an effective portrayal of the unit in the battle.

125 Collison, C.S. *The 11th Royal Warwicks in France 1915-16*. Birmingham:
     Cornish Brothers, 1928. The book is from the diary of the commanding
     officer and covers the fighting from July 1 through mid-August in detail.

126 Coloniales, Section Technique de Troupes. *Historique des Troupes Coloniales
     pendant la Guerre, 1914-1918*. [History of Colonial Troops During the War,
     1914-1918.] Paris: Lavauzelle, 1923. Provides account of colonial forces
     which were part of the initial French assault on July 1.

127 Committee of Officers Who Served with the Battalion. *The War History of the
     Sixth Battalion The South Staffordshire Regiment*. London: Heinemann,
     1925. Attacked at Gommecourt on July 1 and found the wire not cut.
     Suffered very heavy casualties, and the authors suggest the attack was of little
     value.

128 Congreve, Billy. *Armageddon Road: A VC's Diary, 1914-1916*. Edited by
     Terry Norman. London: William Kimber, 1882. The son of General Walter

Congreve (XIII Corps at the Somme) Billy Congreve was a promising young officer with the Rifle Brigade. He was killed in the trenches on July 20. The account of Billy's activities at the Somme provides an example of the fate of an officer in routine daily operations.

129   Cooksey, Jon. *Pals: The 13th and 14th (Service) Battalions (Barnsley) The York and Lancaster Regiment*. Barnsley: Warncliffe, 1986. These two Battalions were with the 94th Brigade, 31st Division, which attacked at Serre on July 1. Their casualties were extreme. This is an account of one of the worst situations of the attack.

130   Coop, J.O. *The Story of the 55th (West Lancashire) Division*. Liverpool: Daily Post Printers, 1919. Coop describes the activity of the 55th Division, which was in action at the Somme for most of September, including the battles of Guillemont, Ginchy, Flers-Courcelette, and Morval.

131   Cooper, Alfred Duff. *Haig*. 2 Vols. London: Faber and Faber, 1935-36. This study is very heavily based on the typed version of Haig's diary and on his letters, but is valuable as presentation of Haig's views.

132   Coppard, George. *With a Machine Gun to Cambrai*. London: Her Majesty's Stationery Office, 1969. Coppard was a private and is bitterly critical of attack-ing against superior defenses. Artillery preparation often failed and troops should not have been committed till it was known that the wire was cut.

133   Coreda, M.L.V.H. *La Guerre Mondiale, 1914-1918*. [The World War, 1914-1918.] Paris: Chapelot, 1922. Solid account from the French view and quite fair to the British, crediting them with saving Verdun. Not always accurate in detail, however.

134   Corrigall, D. J. *The History of the Twentieth Canadian Battalion (Central Ontario Regiment) Canadian Expeditionary Force in the Great War, 1914-1918*. Toronto: Stone and Cox, 1935. Corrigall provides a detailed description of the Battalion's activities at Flers-Courcelette, Thiepval, and Ancre Heights during the last three months of the Somme offensive. He offers little comment or analysis, however.

135   Coultass, Clive. "Film as an Historical Source: Its Use and Abuse." *Archives* 8 (1977): 12-19. Examination of newsreels from the Battle of the Somme, showing misrepresentations.

136   Cousine, A. *La 42e D.I. Mémorie de Maîtrise*. [The 42nd Infantry Division: Memories of Mastery.] Paris: Sorbonne, 1969. Includes account of the unit near Rancourt in September and Sailly-Saillisel in October and November.

137 Cowley, Robert. "The Bloodiest Battle in History." *Horizon* 14 (1972): 116-119. Criticizes the choice of ground and strategic goals of the Somme and suggests the loss of a generation.

138 Cramm, Richard. *First Five Hundred: Being a Historical Sketch of the Military Operations of the Royal Newfoundland Regiment in Gallipoli and on the Western Front.* Albany: C.F. Williams and Son, 1921. Provides account of the Newfoundlanders who were virtually wiped out in a futile July 1 attack that, had communications been better, would not have been launched.

139 Creagh, O'Moore, and E.M. Humphris, eds. *The VC and DSO.* 3 Vols London: Standard Art Book Co., n.d. Listing of every winner of the VC and DSO from the Crimean War to the end of World War I with biographical sketches and photos.

140 Croft, John, "The Somme: 14 July 1916--A Great Opportunity Missed?" *Army Quarterly and Defense Journal* 116 (July, 1986): 312-320. Author suggests that there was an opportunity for use of cavalry to exploit a British breakthrough. Failure to do so cost the allies a major victory.

141 Croft, W.D. *Three Years with the 9th (Scottish) Division.* London: John Murray, 1919. Croft's solid account illustrates the communications problems of the British in 1916. At the beginning of the offensive, the 9th Division was to make a follow-up attack on Montauban, got lost (which helped the unit avoid an evening under shell fire), and ended up attacking Bernafay Wood rather than its assigned target. The Division also fought at Longueval in mid-July.

142 Croney, Percy. *Soldier's Luck: Memoirs of the Great War.* Ilfracombe: Arthur H. Stockwell, 1965. The author was with the 1st Essex, and fought at the Somme near Beaumont Hamel where he was wounded. His description of the battle lacks context, and so it is most useful for details of combat.

143 Crookenden, Arthur. *The History of the Cheshire Regiment in the Great War.* 2nd ed. Chester: W.H. Evans and Sons, 1939. Author notes some revisions in second edition, most concerning events in 1915. Concerning the Somme, recounts combat by battalions of the regiment in most of the major actions from July through November.

144 Cross, Robin. *The Bombers: The Illustrated Story of Offensive Strategy and Tactics in the Twentieth Century.* New York: Macmillan, 1987. Provides an account of efforts to interdict German logistics and communications during the Somme.

145   Crozier, F.P. *A Brass-hat in No Man's Land.* London: Jonathan Cape, 1930.
      Autobiographical account including service with the Ulster Division and the
      attack on Thiepval in the first days of July.

146   Crozier, F.P. *The Men I Killed.* London: Michael Joseph, 1937. Although
      mostly an attack on war in terms of the 1930s appeasers, there are comments
      about the use of force to maintain combat discipline at the Somme, at which
      Crozier was an officer with the 36th Division. These comments make the
      book of some interest to students of the battle.

147   Cru, Jean Norton. *Témoins.* [Witnesses.] Paris: Les Etincelles, 1929. This
      study of eyewitness accounts of World War I included more than 300
      examples. It was published in a modified and shortened version as *Du
      Témoignage.* Paris: Librairie Gallimard, 1931; and in English as *War Books:
      A Study in Historical Criticism.* Translated and edited by Stanley J. Pincetl,
      Jr. and Ernest Marchand. San Diego: San Diego State University Press,
      1976. Cru's analysis of personal accounts from diaries to autobiographical
      novels is powerful and deserves attention even though the number of French
      accounts of the Somme is low.

148   Crutchley, C.E., ed. *Machine Gunner, 1914-1918: Personal Experiences of the
      Machine Gun Corps.* 2nd ed. Folkstone: Bailey Brothers and Swinfen, 1975;
      orig. 1973. Short personal accounts of varying value of the Somme campaign
      from July through November.

149   Cruttwell, C.R.M.F. *A History of the Great War. Oxford:* Oxford University
      Press, 1934; 2nd ed. 1936. One of the best accounts of the war. Mildly
      critical of Haig and other generals at the Somme, Cruttwell suggests the main
      problems were failure of bombardment to cut wire and destroy defenses;
      attacking well after sun-up so assault force could be easily seen; and attacking
      on so broad a front.

150   Cruttwell, C.R.M.F. *The Role of British Strategy in the Great War.* Cambridge:
      Cambridge University Press, 1936. The author condemns the British Cabinet
      for being dilatory and failing to exert much control over strategy before 1917.
      He also makes an eloquent defense of the thinking of the Easterners, although
      he does not agree with the specific suggestions of Lloyd George and
      Churchill.   Concerning the Somme, he suggests that Haig's idea of a
      breakthrough as if the front were a fort was negated by the availability of
      reserves and that limited attacks were preferable. He acknowledges that the
      offensive hurt German morale, but thinks the withdrawal to the Hindenburg
      Line in 1917 eliminated all practical gains by the attackers.

151   Cruttwell, C.R.M.F. *The War Service of the 1/4 Royal Berkshire Regiment.*

Oxford: Basil Blackwell, 1922. The history of a battalion offers a limited canvass for a historian. Cruttwell, one of the best of his generation, provides the context and carefully done maps that make the situation clear. His account of the unit's action around Pozières in July and August is excellent.

152   Cuddeford, D.W.J. *And All for What? Some War Time Experiences*. London: Heath Cranton, 1933. Although Cuddeford, who served with the Scots Guards, gives a very personal account, he does offer some interesting comments about life in the trenches and combat. His unit was part of the attack on Martinpuich in September.

153   Cuneo, John R. *Winged Mars*. 2 Vols. Harrisburg: Military Service Publishing Co., 1942; rpt. 1947. Provides account of the German air force's difficult struggle to counter Anglo-French air superiority over the Somme.

154   Cunliffe, Marcus. *The Royal Irish Fusiliers*. London: Oxford University Press, 1952. Cunliffe provides accounts of battalions of Irish Fusiliers involvement at Thiepval, Combles Trench, Guillemont, and Ginchy.

155   D'Almeida, P. Camena. *L'Armée Allemande Avant et Pendant La Guerre de 1914-1918*. [The German Army before and during the War of 1914-1918.] Paris: Berger-Levrault, 1919. Detailed military history including organization and unit activity down to the level of regiments.

156   Daniell, David Scott. *Cap of Honour: The Story of the Gloucester Regiment (The 28th/61st Foot) 1694-1975*. London: White Lion Publishing, 1951. In covering such an extended period in a single volume, Daniell can give only brief descriptions of events. He does, however, manage to outline effectively the unit's involvement in the July 15th night attack at Contalmaison.

157   *Das Infanterie Regiment 66 im Weltkrieg*. [The 66th Infantry Regiment in the World War.] Berlin: Kalk, 1930. Provides account of German unit involved in the defense of Thiepval.

158   *Das K.B. 10 Infanterie Regiment König*. [The 10th Royal Bavarian Infantry Regiment.] Munich: Bayerisches Kriegsarchiv, 1925. Official history of a unit brought into the defense against the British attacks of September 15.

159   Davson, H.M. *The History of the 35th Division in the Great War*. London: Sifton Praed and Co., 1927. With a brief exception, the Division did not act as a unit at the Somme. Brigades from it fought at Waterlot Farm and Maltz Horn Farm on July 18th, and two of its brigades were at Bernafay Wood on July 19th with many casualties and little to show for them. It did attack as a whole at Guillemont on the 21st, but this did not come off well. The 35th was

a Bantam Division (men 5' to 5' 3"), but the experiment of using undersized soldiers failed after the first effort as the quality of the recruits declined. In December, 1916, 2,784 men were declared unfit for duty in thirteen days, and the reduced height standard was then abolished.

160 Dawson, A.J. *Somme Battle Stories*. London: Hodder and Stoughton, 1916. The stories included are mostly far fetched, but there are good illustrations by Bruce Bairnsfather.

161 Dawson, C. *Carry On*. Toronto: Gundy, 1917. Dawson, a Canadian, provides an account of the horrors of the Somme and much praise of the rank and file.

162 Delmain, Frank, ed. *Going Across or With the 9th Welsh in the Butterfly Division, Being Extracts from the War Letters and Diary of Lieut. M. St. Helier Evans*. Newport: R.H. Johns, n.d. Articulate account of trench life at the Somme in 1916 but little description of fighting.

163 Denman, Terence. *Ireland's Unknown Soldiers: The 16th (Irish) Division in the Great War, 1914-1918*. Dublin: Irish Academic Press, 1992. Denman's purpose is to record the heroism of the Catholic nationalist Irish soldiers in the war, and especially at Guillemont and Ginchy during the Somme offensive. He did not allow ideology to prevent him from writing an effective account of the 16th Division's activities, however.

164 Deutelmoser, Major. *Die 27 Infanterie-Division im Weltkrieg 1914-18*. [The 27th Infantry Division in the World War, 1914-1918.] Stuttgart: Berger, 1925. Division held Guillemont for most of August enduring heavy British attacks and shelling. Author offers testimony to the impact of the barrage.

165 Devine, W. *Story of a Battalion*. Melbourne: Melville and Mullen, 1919. The Battalion in this account is the 48th, which was engaged near Courcelette in August.

166 Dewar, George A.B. with J.H. Boraston. *Sir Douglas Haig's Command, December 19, 1915 to November 11, 1918*. 2 Vols. London: Constable, 1922. The authors are very pro-Haig, and defend the general against almost every criticism made of him, including the use of tanks. The failure on July 1 was due to inexperience, inadequate training, and inadequate supply of guns and shells due to lack of production. They blame the weather for failure in October. They list three goals for the Somme: relieving Verdun, keeping German troops from going East, and wearing down the foe, and deny that there was any geographical goal at all.

167 Dieppe, Clive, ed. *As It Was: A Graphic Frontline Record in Pictures, the*

Majority Never Before Published, of our Diggers and their Foe on the Western Front 1916-1918. Sydney: Wentworth Books, 1973. This photographic history is made much more valuable by the editor's decision to include pictures of the Germans, often arranging the scenes to juxtapose similar activities by the men of the two sides.

168 Dillon, The *Viscount. Memoirs of Three Wars*. London: Allan Wingate, 1951. Provides picture of Allied relations during the battle and an example of rear echelon optimism.

169 Dinning, Hector. *By-ways on Service: Notes from an Australian Journal*. London: Constable, 1918. The author was behind the lines at the Somme, but his description of a casualty clearing station, logistical efforts, and the aftermath of battle are instructive.

170 Dolden, A.S. *Cannon Fodder: An Infantryman's Life on the Western Front, 1914-1918*. Poole, Dorset: Blandford Press, 1980. Based on author's day to day diary kept during the war. Dolden was a cook, and so although his battalion (part of the 168th Brigade) attacked on the left of Gommecourt Wood on July 1, he did not participate in the fighting. He did draw some front line duty, and describes conditions fairly well.

171 Dollman, Walter, and H.M. Skinner. *The Blue and Brown Diamond, A History of the 27th Battalion, Australian Imperial Force, 1915-1919*. Adelaide: Lonnen and Cope, 1921. The authors, an interesting combination of a lieutenant colonel and a sergeant, describe the activity of their battalion which fought at the Somme, notably near Courcelette in early August.

172 Douie, Charles. *The Weary Road: Recollections of a Subaltern of Infantry*. London: John Murray, 1929. An account of the Dorset Regiment, which fought at Thiepval in the first attacks and then in November at Serre Ridge. The accounts were originally published in The Nineteenth Century and After.

173 Doyle, Arthur Conan. *The British Campaign in Europe*. London: Bles, 1928. A revised version of Doyle's British Campaigns in France and Flanders.

174 Doyle, Arthur Conan. *The British Campaigns in France and Flanders*. 6 Vols. London: Hodder and Stoughton, 1916-20. The author devotes volume three to 1916 in France and Flanders, and gives a detailed account of the battle. He praises the English, including production workers back home, and suggests that the Germans were battered and knew it. This is a very nationalistic account.

175 Dugmore, A. Radclyffe. *When the Somme Ran Red*. New York: George H.

Doran Co., 1918. Eyewitness account of soldier with the King's Own Yorkshire Light Infantry following the author's experiences through early July when he was wounded and no longer fit for active service.

176 Duguid, A. Fortescue. *Official History of the Canadian Forces in the Great War 1914-1919.* Ottawa: King's Printer, 1938. Useful for details of the Canadians at the Somme, where their divisions fought from September until the end of the offensive.

177 Duncan, G.S. *Douglas Haig as I Knew Him.* London: George Allen and Unwin, 1966. The author was Haig's chaplain during much of the war and offers useful insight into the general's character.

178 Dundas, R.N. *Henry Dundas Scots Guard: A Memoir.* Edinburgh: William Blackwood and Sons, 1921. This volume is made up of Dundas's letters organized and tied together by his father. It gives a picture of a young, inexperienced officer in the 1st Battalion of the Scots Guards. His picture of fighting at the Somme, in September near Guillemont and at Les Boeufs, is conventional but clear.

179 Eden, Anthony (Earl of Avon). *Another World, 1897-1917.* London: Lane, 1976. Eden was a junior officer with the Yeoman Rifles in the 41st Division. He provides an upper-class Englishman's point-of-view of the war and the Somme, where his unit was part of the September attacks.

180 Edmonds, Charles [Charles E. Carrington.] *A Subaltern's War.* London: Davies, 1929. A classic account of the war by an officer who served with the 48th Division at the Somme.

181 Edmonds, James. *A Short History of World War I.* London: Oxford University Press, 1951. An excellent survey covering all campaigns, but because of the author's emphasis on land war and the Western Front, it is particularly good for the study of the Somme offensive.

182 Edmonds, John, et al. *Military Operations: France and Belgium.* 14 Vols. London: Macmillan, 1922-40; His Majesty's Stationery Office, 1941-49. Volumes 5 (1932) and 6 (1938) concern 1916. This official history is filled with detailed factual information, some of which is not found anywhere else except in archives. Its interpretations, however, have been questioned. Edmonds, according to some, insisted on an interpretation that was unreasonably supportive of Haig and General Headquarters, and hence tending to blame subordinates.

183 Edmunds, G.B. *Somme Memories of an Australian Artillery Driver,*

1916-1919. Ilfracombe: Stockwell, 1955. First hand account of an Australian unit.

184 Ellis, A.D. *The Story of the Fifth Australian Division.* London: Hodder and Stoughton, [1920.] The 5th did not reach the Somme until October, but then held the line near Flers. The history of the Division in this period provides a description of the conclusion of the offensive and the effort to consolidate its gains.

185 Ellis, Hugh, et al. *Fighting Tanks: An Account of the Royal Tank Corps in Action 1916-1919.* London: Seeley, Service and Co., 1929. Includes account of tanks in September, 1916, with personal experiences written by the commander of one machine. Asserts that by using tanks at the Somme "the surprise was allowed to fizzle out like a cheap rocket. . . ."

186 Ellis, John. *Eye Deep in Hell: Trench Warfare in World War I.* London: Croom Helm, 1976. Using an excellent balance of photographs and text, Ellis gives a real sense of what a soldier's life on the Western Front was like. His book is a valuable supplement to any study of battle in the war.

187 English, John A. *On Infantry.* New York: Praeger, 1981; rev. ed. 1994. English provides a valuable overview of infantry tactics in the 20th century. Concerning World War I, he was influenced by Liddell Hart and tends not to give the British army its due.

188 Enser, A.G.S. *A Subject Bibliography of the First World War: Books in English 1914-1987.* 2nd ed. Brookfield, VT: Gower, 1990; orig. 1979. Enser has provided a useful reference for those seeking a general bibliography of the war. His book is hard to use if a specific book or a subject not among his headings is sought. He provides only thirty references under Somme and since there are no cross references it would be hard to expand the list from his entries.

189 Etzer, H. *Das K.B. 9, Infanterie Regiment.* [The 9th Royal Bavarian Infantry Regiment.] Munich: Schick, 1928. Etzer provides a good description of the effect of the British attack and the German defense in September.

190 Ewart, Wilfrid. *Scots Guard.* London: Rich and Cowan, 1934. This volume, the second of the author's papers to be published, is the reminiscences of a regimental officer in France. It also includes an account of a return visit to the Somme battlefield in 1919.

191 Ewing, John. *The History of the 9th (Scottish) Division 1914-1919.* London: John Murray, 1921. The 9th was involved in the capture of Bernafay Wood

and fight for Trônes Wood. July 14-18 it fought at Longueval, defeating German counter-attack on the 18th. It was relieved on the 19th.

192 Ewing, John. *The Royal Scots 1914-1919*. 2 Vols. Edinburgh: Oliver and Boyd, 1925. Solid account of the activities of the battalions of the regiment which were involved in most of the major actions of the Somme campaign.

193 Eyre, Giles E.M. *Somme Harvest: Memories of a P.B.I. in the Summer of 1916*. London: Jarrolds, 1938; rpt. 1991. Erye provides a detailed though quite personal account of battle. His book is useful for atmosphere but not analysis.

194 Fabry, Jean J. *Joffre et son Destin*. [Joffre and his Destiny.] Paris: Charles Lavauzelle, 1932. This account is very favorable to Joffre. It asserts that 1916 was a disaster for the Germans and refers to Haig and Robertson as Joffre's best assistants. The discussion is of strategy and not of the battle itself.

195 Fairclough, J.E.B. *The First Birmingham Battalion in the Great War, 1914-1915*. Birmingham: Cornish Brothers, 1933. In reserve at first, the Battalion entered the fighting on July 22 and took such heavy casualties in an attack at Longueval on July 30 that it was relieved. In September it fought at Falfemont and Morval. This is a first person account.

196 Falkenhayn, Erich von. *General Headquarters, 1914-1916*. London: Hutchinson, 1919. The German general remarks that, although Allied propaganda, including its assertion that the Somme was a disaster for the German Army, had a deleterious impact in Germany, in fact, he did not think that the battle hurt the Germans badly, certainly not in proportion to the losses of the Entente. Also provides useful information about the defense effort in the beginning of the Somme offensive.

197 Falkenhayn, General [Erich] von. *The German General Staff and Its Decisions, 1914-1916*. New York: Dodd Mead, 1920. The German general defends the handling of defense at the Somme. Despite heavy losses, Germany was much less harmed than the entente, which "was practically crippled." Although entente propaganda claimed otherwise, the Somme really had little effect on Germany's war effort.

198 Falls, Cyril. *The Great War*. New York: Capricorn Books, 1959. Excellent and even handed account of the war. Falls, unlike his contemporaries Liddell Hart and Cruttwell, served to the end of the war and was more inclined to see the stalemate of 1916 as prelude to victory in 1917 and 1918. Title for British publication is *The First World War*.

199 Falls, Cyril. *The History of the First Seven Battalions the Royal Irish Rifles in the Great War.* 2 Vols. Aldershot: Gale and Polden, 1925. At Ovillers on July 1, two battalions fell at their own front lines. The attack was resumed by other battalions on July 7 and 15. Falls notes that counter-battery work was inadequate. Irish rifles fought again at Ginchy in September and later at the Ancre. Falls, an excellent professional historian, gives a good account.

200 Falls, Cyril. *The History of the 36th (Ulster) Division.* London: McCaw, Stevenson and Orr, 1922. The author is one of the better historians of World War I of the first half of the 20th century. His account of the Ulster Division, which particularly distinguished itself at Thiepval on July 1, is excellent.

201 Falls, Cyril. *Life of a Regiment: The Gordon Highlanders in the First World War.* Aberdeen: Aberdeen University Press, 1958. Effective unit history by a good historian. Gordon Highlanders were engaged particularly at Beaumont Hamel.

202 Falls, Cyril. *Marshal Foch.* London: Blackie, 1939. This short biography of the commander of the French forces at the Somme is useful because of the quality of the author's work. Space devoted to the Somme is limited.

203 Falls, Cyril. *War Books: A Critical Guide.* London: Peter Davies, 1930; rpt. 1989. Although dated, Falls' acute comments make this bibliography valuable. It is well organized and easy to use.

204 Farndale, M. *History of the Royal Regiment of Artillery: Western Front 1914-1918.* Woolwich: Royal Artillery Institution, 1986. Based on the un-published writing of E.C. Anstey, this volume discusses the importance of artillery for the major battles of the Western Front.

205 Farrar, L.L. "'This Unfathomable Sphinx': German Efforts During 1916 to Con-clude a Separate Peace." *New Review of East-European History* 15 (June 1975): 65-90. German efforts to break up the Entente by making separate peace deals failed due to Verdun and the Somme.

206 Farrar-Hockley, Anthony H. *Goughie: The Life of General Sir Hubert Gough.* London: Hart-Davis, MacGibbon, 1975. At first in command of the reserve, on the evening of July 1 Gough was given command of the two corps on the British left. He cancelled orders to renew the general attack but carried on the campaign with carefully prepared limited assaults. Author has a clearly positive opinion of his subject.

207 Farrar-Hockley, Anthony H. *The Somme.* London: Batsford, 1964. Overall the best account of the battle. The author tends to blame Haig for poor planning

but makes frequent comments on poor communications and command control during the battle, most aspects of which were out of Haig's control. He also criticizes Haig for pushing the latter parts of the battle so as to improve his position with the politicians at home and in allied conferences planning the 1917 campaign. Farrar-Hockley maintains there were three lost opportunities: July 1 at Montauban; July 14 at High Wood; and September 15 at Flers when if used en masse tanks might have created a breakthrough.

208 Feilding, Rowland. *War Letters to A Wife: France and Flanders, 1915-1919.* London: Medici Society, 1929. Author was a Guards officer and behind the lines until September 10 when, having taken command of the 6th Battalion, Connaught Rangers, he led the battered unit in an attack on Ginchy. His letters are mostly personal comments but have value for eyewitness details of the situation.

209 Fetherstonhaugh, Robert C., ed. *The Royal Montreal Regiment: 14th Battalion, C.E.F.* Montreal: Gazette Printing Co., 1927. Account of a Canadian unit in action around Mouquet Farm, Courcelette, and Regina Trench in September and October. In about five weeks some 600 men were killed.

210 Fetherstonhaugh, Robert C. *The 24th Battalion, C.E.F., Victoria Rifles of Canada.* Montreal: Gazette Printing Co., 1930. Well-written account of Canadian unit which saw much action in late September and early October at Regina Trench.

211 Filgate, J. Macartney. *The History of the 33rd Division Artillery in the War, 1914-1918.* London: Vacher and Sons, 1921. Accounts of artillerymen are somewhat rare, and the 33rd Division fought at Albert, Bazentin Ridge, and High Wood during the first month of the Somme offensive.

212 Fletcher, C.R.L. *The Great War, 1914-1918.* London: John Murray, 1920. Well-written survey best used for descriptions of the tactical situation.

213 Fletcher, David. *Tanks and Trenches: First Hand Accounts of Tank Warfare in the First World War.* London: MBI-Alan Sutton, 1995. Heavily illustrated account of the birth and early development of tanks including their introduction at Flers-Courcelette in September during the Somme offensive.

214 Fletcher, D.J. "The Origins of Armour." *In Armoured Warfare*, ed. J.P. Harris and F.H. Toase. London: Batsford, 1990. A pro-tank discussion of World War I armor usage.

215 Foch, Ferdinand. *The Memoirs of Marshal Foch.* Translated by T. Bentley Mott. London: Heinemann, 1931. Foch commanded the French forces involved in

the Somme offensive but gives more attention to the beginning and end of the war when he was more prominent. Although he discusses the Somme in a number of contexts, his account of the battle itself takes only a few pages.

216 Forbes, A.F. *A History of the Army Ordnance Services*. 3 Vols. London: Medici Society, 1929. Logistics is the essential background for any military operation, and ordnance supply for the Somme offensive was a major concern.

217 Forde, Frank. "Tyneside Irish Brigade." *Irish Sword* 16 (1985): 117-122. Description of unit decimated in July 1 attack and rebuilt.

218 Foulkes, C.H. *"Gas!" The Story of the Special Brigade*. Edinburgh: William Blackwood and Sons, 1934. Foulkes was in charge of the British effort to develop military gases and a strong advocate of the weapon. He continued to favor discharge from cylinders in the trenches even after this method resulted in problems due to shifting winds at Loos in 1915. He is critical of the decision to use gas as part of the preliminary bombardment at the Somme rather than just before the assault and dismisses the fears of infantry officers of the effects of gas on the attackers.

219 Fox, Frank. *The Royal Inniskilling Fusiliers in the World War*. London: Constable, 1928. Includes accounts of fighting at the Crucifix Line on July 1 when the Fusiliers were forced to yield gains due to lack of resupply and at Ovillers on July 9 when objective was taken and held. Fusiliers were also in action at Guillemont and Ginchy in early September.

220 France. *L'Aeronautique pendant le Guerre Mondiale*. [Aeronautics During the World War.] Paris: Maurice de Brunoff, 1919. This volume of official history presents the Somme as a wonderful period for the French air force during which patrols were well organized, but individual aces were still able to act on their own.

221 France. Ministère de la Guerre. État-Major de l'Armée. Service Historique. *Les Armées françaises dan la Grande Guerre*. [General Staff of the Army His-torical Service. The Armies of France in the Great War.] 11 tomes. Paris, Imprimerie Nationale, 1922-37. Like the British official history, the French is a massive accumulation of detailed information. It has, however, been superseded by more modern accounts. The material concerning the Somme is in Tome 4.

222 French, Anthony. *Gone for a Soldier*. Kineton: Roundwood Press, 1972. This volume is a short memoir of the war including an attack near High Wood in September. The most interesting element is an account of a harrowing two days in no man's land after being wounded.

223   French, David. *British Strategy and War Aims*. London: Allen and Unwin, 1986. French does an excellent job of setting strategic decision making into political, diplomatic and economic context and establishing that the decision to undertake the Somme offensive was part of a larger aim to ultimately be able to impose peace on friend and foe alike.

224   French, David. "The Meaning of Attrition 1914-1916." *English Historical Review* 103 (1988): 385-405. The experience of the Somme gave the word "attrition" its negative connotation.

225   Fuller, J.F.C. *Tanks in the Great War*. London: John Murray, 1920. Fuller, who became one of the important advocates of tanks between the wars, details their use at the Somme. Using the machines in small groups to take-out strong points did not work well on September 15 and too many bogged down in the mud on September 25-26 and November 13-14 to represent a reasonable test. The occasional successes on these occasions showed the promise of the weapon, especially if the lessons learned resulted in mechanical improvement and better command control. Fuller supports the decision to use them.

226   Fyfe, Albert J. *Understanding the First World War*. Vol. 37 of Series IX: History, American University Studies. New York: Peter Lang, 1988. Fyfe is critical of Haig and Rawlinson arguing that the Somme was a poor choice of ground for an offensive and that neither general had confidence in his men to take the initiative. The latter attitude caused the use of rigid formations resulting in higher than necessary casualties. He also faults Rawlinson for failing to reinforce success. Overall the book reiterates most of the criticisms that have been made of the offensive over the years.

227   Gallini, J. *Essai de rupture du front en 1916. Les attaques des 1er, 2 et 3 juillet dans la Somme*. [Attempt to Break the Front in 1916. The Attacks of the 1st, 2nd and 3rd of July on the Somme.] Paris: Charles Lavauzelle, 1939. Gallini provides a useful account of fighting at the Somme and especially the French involvement.

228   Gallini, J. "Joffre et la Somme." [Joffre and the Somme.] *Revue d'Histoire de la Guerre Mondiale* 4 (1936): 305-43. This article provides a French perspective of the dispute over Joffre's involvement in the decision making about the Somme offensive.

229   Gallini, J. "Les Premiers pas du char britannique: la bataille du 15 septembre 1916." [The First Move of British Tanks: The Battle of September 15, 1916.] *Revue d'Infanterie* (mars, avril, et mai, 1939), 521-32, 739-68, 932-65. Gallini, a French army officer, provides a detailed analysis of the first use of

tanks.

230   Gallwitz, Max von. *Erleben in Westen 1916-1918*. [Experiences on the Western Front, 1916-1918.] Berlin: E.S. Mittler und Sohn, 1928. General Gallwitz was brought from Verdun to take over the Second Army. He reorganized defenses and artillery, but did not get reinforcements which were sent to the East instead. In his account, Gallwitz refers to the Somme as "a lost battle."

231   Gambier F., and M. Suire. *Histoire de la Première Guerre Mondiale*. [History of the First World War.] 2 Vols. Paris: Fayard, 1968. Like most French military histories, this volume gives relatively little attention to the Somme, although the battle is described. The authors conclude that Joffre intended to continue the push in 1917 and did not consider the limited gains an overall failure.

232   Gammage, Bill. *The Broken Years: Australian Soldiers in the Great War*. Canberra: Australian National University Press, 1974. A very good Australian account of the battle from Pozières in late July to December. The focus in the book is on the soldiers.

233   Gardner, Brian. *The Big Push: A Portrait of the Somme*. London: Cassell, 1961. Notes low quality of English officers--low pay drew those who had failed at other sorts of education to military training. Criticizes Haig's plan for depending on success of initial artillery barrage to break open the front. Furthermore, cavalry was expected to dash through without much attention to the possibility of the Germans might create a pocket and trap the horsemen. Speaks ill of Joffre for pushing for battle of attrition at the Somme to pull Germans from Verdun, though he does admit that the original plan predated the attack at Verdun. Criticizes Haig for pushing the later part of the offensive to help himself politically in the face of criticism at home and at the meetings to plan for the 1917 campaign.

234   Gehre, Ludwig. *Die deutsche Kräftverteilung Während des Weltkriege*. [German Distribution of Forces during the World War.] Berlin: E.S. Mittler und Sohn, 1928. Gehre suggests that the renewed offensive at Verdun in August was an effort to draw entente forces from the Somme and that the Germans were mistaken to try to fight at both places.

235   Gengler, Ludwig. *Rudolf Berthold*. Berlin: Schlieffen, 1934. Biography of flyer who served with the German air corps over the Somme.

236   Germains, Victor W. *The Kitchener Armies*. London: Peter Davies, 1930. Good account of the Somme campaign, which the author sees as the destruction of Britain's tradition of volunteer forces.

237   Gerster, Mattäus. *Die Schwaben an der Ancre*. [The Swabians at the Ancre.] Heilbron: Salzer, 1920. Eyewitness account by a member of the German 26th Reserve Division. Describes July 1 well. Comments on the leisurely approach of the British attack, as if they did not expect opposition and notes the courage shown.

238   Gerster, Mattäus. *Das Württemberg Reserve Infanterie Regiment Nr. 119 im Weltkrieg, 1914-1918*. [The 119th Wurtemberg Reserve Infantry Regiment in the World War, 1914-1918.] Stuttgart: Belser, 1920. Useful German unit history by a veteran who served at the Somme.

239   Gibbs, Philip. *The Battles of the Somme*. London: Heinemann, 1917. This book is a compilation of Gibbs' news articles written while covering the battle. He notes his wish to reveal the valor and sacrifice of the English soldier.

240   Gibbs, Philip. *The Germans on the Somme*. London: Darling and Son, 1917. Really a pamphlet about how terrible the battle was for the Germans. No indication of how Gibbs might know about the enemy. More useful as an example of British propaganda than as a study of the Germans.

241   Gibbs, Philip. *Now It Can Be Told*. New York: Harper and Brothers, 1920. Gibbs claims to portray the realities of war here, noting that his earlier publications, though true, were censored. He recounts what he witnessed at the Somme, with comments about heroism, futility, etc. The book is really more important as a statement of postwar disillusionment than as account of battle.

242   Gibson, R. and P. Oldfield. City: *The 12th (Service) Battalion (Sheffield) The York and Lancaster Regiment*. Barnsley: Warncliffe, 1988. Attacked at Serre on July 1 as part of 94th Brigade, 31st Division. This is an account of one of the truly horrific situations of the attack--casualties were terrible.

243   Gilbert, Martin. *Atlas of World War I*. 2nd ed. New York: Oxford University Press, 1994. Gilbert provides an excellent layout of the geographical situation of all campaigns in the war. The maps are clear and easily read.

244   Gilbert, Martin. *The Challenge of War: 1914-1916*. Vol 3, *Winston Churchill*. London: Heinemann, 1971. Narrative account of Churchill's involvement in the "Easterner" versus "Westerner" debate over strategy that led up to the Somme. Gilbert, Churchill's official biographer, offers little analysis.

245   Gilbert, Martin. *The First World War: A Complete History*. New York: Henry Holt, 1994. Excellent survey of the war with two chapters devoted largely to

the Somme campaign.

246   Giles, John. *The Somme Then and Now*. London: Bailey Brothers and Swinfen, 1977; rev. ed. 1986. The text of this book is no more than an outline description of the campaign, but the numerous photographs--many contemporary with the battle--make it well worth consulting.

247   Gillon, Stair. *The K.O.S.B.* [King's Own Scottish Borderers] *in the Great War*. London: Thomas Nelson and Sons, 1930. Accounts are divided by battalion and include descriptions of fighting at the Ancre and Bernafay Wood on July 1, Delville Wood on August 14, and Martinpuich on September 15. Although episodic, this volume is well done.

248   Gillon, Stair. *The Story of the 29th Division*. London: Thomas Nelson and Sons, 1925. Already famed for its efforts in Gallipoli, the 29th Division attacked, on July 1, with Beaumont Hamel as its objective. The Newfoundland regiment was sacrificed, attacking through paths in the wire which were targeted by German machine guns. The Division took some 5,000 casualties. It was relieved but did return to the Somme fighting in October near Flers.

249   Girard, Georges. *La Bataille de la Somme en 1916*. [The Battle of the Somme in 1916.] Paris: Charles Lavauzelle, 1937. Unfortunately the author has chosen to base his work heavily on the French official history, which is little more than a summary of government documents. The result is that tactical considerations are virtually ignored. He regards the French effort as merely flank support for the British and praises Haig for perseverance. He argues that had Joffre remained in command the offensive would have been renewed in 1917 and the war won.

250   Girard, Georges. *Sur le Front occidental avec la 53e Division d'Infanterie*. [On the Western Front with the 53rd Infantry Division.] 2 Vols. Bescançon: Sequania, 1936. The author, an artilleryman, fought at the Somme from May to August, 1916, and provides a pedestrian and unsurprising account of his experiences.

251   Gladden, Norman. *The Somme 1916: A Personal Account*. London: William Kimber, 1974. Based on the author's diary. He was mostly in support during the Somme battles but did see some combat. This the account of a shy boy who did not much care for the experience of soldering.

252   "Glendower." "Haig and Tanks." *Army Quarterly* 96 (April-July 1968): 197-202. The author defends Haig, noting the general's early interest (1915) in tanks, ordering them tested at the Somme, and then ordering 1,000.

253   Gliddon, Gerald. *V.C.s of the Somme: A Biographical Portrait*. Norwich:
      Gliddon, 1991. Brief biographical studies of the men who won Victoria
      Crosses at the battle of the Somme.

254   Gliddon, Gerald. *When the Barrage Lifts: A Topographical History and Com-
      mentary on the Battle of the Somme 1916*. London: Leo Cooper, 1987.
      Extremely detailed description breaking the battle down by places. Allows,
      for instance, divisions to be traced to the sites at which they fought.

255   Glubb, John. *Into Battle: A Soldier's Diary of the Great War*. London: Cassell,
      1977. Glubb was a junior officer in the Royal Engineers and gives an in-
      teresting account of the logistical aspects of the struggle from August 5
      through the end of the campaign.

256   Goodspeed, D.J. *The Road Past Vimy*. Toronto: Macmillan, 1969. Goodspeed
      provides a detailed account of the Canadians in action, especially their attacks
      at Courcelette and Regina Trench in the latter half of September.

257   Gorman, Eugene. *"With the Twenty-second," A History of the Twenty-second
      Battalion, A.I.F.* Melbourne: H.H. Champion, 1919. Gorman's battalion, part
      of the 2nd Australian Division, was in action at the Somme, especially in early
      August near Courcelette.

258   Gough, Hubert. *The Fifth Army*. London: Hodder and Stoughton, 1931. Gough
      started the battle as commander of the Reserve Army, intended to exploit
      breakthrough. On the evening of July 1, however, he was given command on
      the left--X and VIII corps. Gough canceled the orders for renewing general
      attack and tried for the rest of the battle to exploit his position on the flank.
      He believed that properly prepared attacks on limited fronts usually worked
      and cited captures of Ovillers and Pozières as evidence. He notes that using
      tanks proved their value and showed defects for correction. Comments on the
      fact that Lloyd George was not supporting Haig and was thinking of other
      fronts--a mistake. Gough believed that the German army was defeated at the
      Somme due to numerous casualties and declining morale, and the Somme was
      the foundation of eventual victory. Overall the book offers a good if standard
      description of the battle.

259   Gough, Hubert. *Soldiering On: Being the Memoirs of General Sir Hubert
      Gough*. London: Arthur Barker, 1954. Minimal comment about the Somme,
      although Gough was in command of the Reserve (5th) Army and after the
      initial attack the left wing.

260   Grafton, C.S. *The Canadian "Emma Gees," A History of the Canadian
      Machine Gun Corps*. Ontario: Canadian Machine Gun Association, 1935.

Provides a description of machine gunners in action at the Somme.

261 Grave, L.W., de. *The War History of the Fifth Battalion the Sherwood Foresters Notts and Derby Regiment 1914-1918.* Derby: Benrose, 1930. Grave provides a step by step account of the July 1 attack at Gommecourt in which the Battalion was badly battered. It was not again committed to the Somme fighting.

262 Graves, Robert. *Goodbye to All That.* London: Jonathan Cape, 1929; numerous reprints. Graves' experience of the Somme was limited due to a serious wound, but his picture of the war, though at times factually inaccurate, is a classic and shows significant military expertise.

263 *The Great Advance: Tales from the Somme Battlefield Told by Wounded Officers and Men on their Arrival at Southampton from the Front.* London: Cassell, 1916. Particularly useful for information about the initial attack and the medical services.

264 Greenwell, Graham H. *An Infant in Arms: War Letters of a Company Officer, 1914-1918.* London: Lovat Dickson and Thompson, 1935; rpt. 1972. Author served with the 4th Oxfordshire and Buckinghamshire Light Infantry in the 48th Division which was heavily engaged at Pozières. His letters give good impression of the horrors of the struggle and indicated that the usual picture of Pozières as an ANZAC show is overstated.

265 Grey, W.E. *2nd City of London Regiment (Royal Fusiliers) in the Great War.* London: Royal Fusiliers, 1929. Competent telling of the deeds and experiences of this territorial unit which served with the 56th Division at Gommecourt, Combles and Le Transloy during the Somme.

266 Grieve, W. Grant, and Bernard Newman. *Tunnellers: The Story of the Tunnelling Companies Royal Engineers, during the World War.* London: Herbert Jenkins, 1936. Accounts, some eyewitness, of the five tunnelling companies working at the Somme.

267 Griffith, Paddy. *Battle Tactics of the Western Front: The British Army's Art of Attack, 1916-18.* New Haven: Yale University Press, 1994. Griffith provides an excellent evaluation of the tactical developments of the war including much discussion of the Somme. His view is somewhat unusual in that he regards the British as more innovative and effectiv e than the Germans. His case is extremely well made.

268 Griffith, Wyn. *Up to Mametz.* London: Faber and Faber, 1931; rpt. 1981. Good account of the initial attack on Mametz Wood by Welsh units, showing the

problems created by inadequate communications with headquarters and the artillery.

269   Gristwood, A.D. *The Somme*. London: Jonathan Cape, 1927. Although a novel, this account of an attack and a soldier's experience of being wounded and evacuated is realistic and effective.

270   Groot, Gerard J. De. *Douglas Haig 1861-1928*. London: Unwin Hyman, 1988. Regards Haig as out of his depth--mired in the cavalry tradition of the 19th century and unable to understand the technological changes in 20th century war.

271   Gudmundsson, Bruce I. *On Artillery*. New York: Praeger, 1993. This study of field artillery, which draws heavily from French and German sources, provides valuable background for the study of the Somme and other battles in World War I.

272   Gudmundsson, Bruce I. *Stormtroop Tactics: Innovation in the German Army 1914-18*. New York: Praeger, 1989. Gudmundsson's study of the Germans is quite good, but by not acknowledging that other armies were developing along the same lines, he leaves too much impression of their superiority.

273   Guinn, Paul. *British Strategy and Politics 1914 to 1918*. Oxford: Clarendon Press, 1965. Guinn argues that military issues from grand strategy to battlefield tactics can only be properly understood in the light of domestic politics. He thoroughly examines the interrelationships of government and military. Chapters 4 and 5 of his book are focused particularly on the Somme.

274   Gwyn, Sandra. *Tapestry of War: A Private View of Canadians in the Great War*. Toronto: Harper Collins, 1992. Although episodic and oddly organized, Gwyn's book does provide some personal details of Canadians and their efforts during the Somme offensive.

275   Haber, L.F. *The Poisonous Cloud: Chemical Warfare in the First World War*. Oxford: Clarendon Press, 1986. Comprehensive survey which sets its brief account of the Somme very usefully into context.

275a   "'Haig' A German Appreciation." *Journal of the Royal United Services Institution* 73 (1928): 226-27. Summary of remarks by General M. von Posek about Haig. Posek says Haig kept on the offensive with clear focus on his objective in battles like the Somme.

276   Haldane, Aylmer. *A Soldier's Saga: The Autobiography of General Sir Aylmer Haldane*. Edinburgh: William Blackwood and Sons, 1948. Haldane, who

commanded the 3rd Division in July and early August, takes credit for the very successful night attack on July 14. Overall, however, this is a pedestrian, possibly self-serving, book and disappointing, for the observations of a divisional commander should provide useful insight into command control and tactical decision making. Haldane fails to do so.

277 Haldane, M.M. *A History of the Fourth Battalion the Seaforth Highlanders*. London: H.F. and G. Witherby, 1928. Brief but well researched accounts of the Battalion's efforts at High Wood in late July and at Beaumont Hamel in November.

278 Hall, Michael. *Sacrifice on the Somme*. Newtownabby: Island Publications, 1993. Pamphlet focused on the Ulster Division at the Somme.

279 Hamilton, Ralph G.A. *The War Diary of the Master of Belhaven 1914-1918*. London: John Murray, 1924. Author was an artillery officer with 106th Brigade, Royal Field Artillery, and fought at the Somme from August through October. Provides an artilleryman's perspective of the battle.

280 Hammerton, John A., ed. *The Great War: I Was There!* 3 Vols. London: The Amalgamated Press, 1938-39. An anthology of participants' accounts of the war including descriptions of the Somme originally published in fifty-one parts.

281 Hammerton, John A.. ed. *A Popular History of the Great War*. 6 Vols. London: Fleetway House, 1934. Descriptive account with little comment.

282 Hare, Steuart. *The Annals of the King's Royal Rifle Corps*. Vol. 5, *The Great War*. London: John Murray, 1932. Unit did not arrive at the Somme until July 15, but after that was involved in most of the major battles of the campaign. Hare's account, going day by day at important points, is well organized and effective.

283 Harris, Henry. *The Irish Regiments in the First World War*. Cork: Mercier Press, 1968. Harris provides a chapter of background and brief accounts of each of the predominantly Irish units at the Somme.

284 Harris, John. *Covenant with Death*. London: Hutchinson, 1961. Fictional but accurate account of recruiting, training, and destruction on July 1 of a battalion in the Kitchener Armies.

285 Harris, John. *The Somme: Death of a Generation*. London: Hodder and Stoughton, 1966; rpt. 1975. Takes most of the traditional critical positions concerning the battle: poor generalship; yielding about location to French

demands; tanks used prematurely; tactics outdated. Does acknowledge that Haig was best British general and that politics were a major factor in forcing the battle.

286 Harris, Ruth Elwin. *Billie: The Neville Letters, 1914-1916*. London: Julia MacRae Books, 1991. The letters of Wilfred Percy "Billie" Neville who served with the 8th East Surrey Regiment in the 18th Division. At the attack on Montauban, July 1, "Billie" had his men dribble foot (soccer) balls across no man's land. He was killed early in the attack, but was an example of the upper class British attitude.

287 Harvey, H.E. *Battle-Line Narratives, 1915-1918*. London: Brentano's Ltd., 1928. Exaggerated tales.

288 Harvey, Norman K. *From Anzac to the Hindenburg Line, The History of the 9th Battalion, A.I.F.* Brisbane: William Brooks, 1941. Detailed unit history of a battalion of the 1st Australian Division including action in the Somme offensive.

289 Harvey, W.J. *The Red and White Diamond*. Melbourne: Alexander McCubbin, [1920.] Harvey, a sergeant, provides an interesting account of the 24th Battalion (2nd Australian Division) which fought at Pozières and Mouquet Farm in July and August.

290 Hauge, Anton. "Slaget Ved Somme." [The Battle of the Somme.] *Samtiden* 72 (1963): 356-63. Reviews British effort and suggests battle should have been broken off after the first day. Commanders lacked common sense.

291 Hawker, Tyrrel Mann. *Hawker V.C.: The Biography of the Late Lanoe George Hawker*. London: Mitre Press, 1965. Hawker commanded R.F.C. Squadron 60 which was at the Somme. This biography provides good coverage including the work on air spotting for counter-battery artillery fire.

292 Hawkings, Frank. *From Ypres to Cambrai: The Diary of an Infantryman, 1914-1919*. Edited by Arthur Taylor. Morley, Yorkshire: Elmfield Press, 1973. Hawkings was in the Queen's Victoria Rifles, 56th Division, and part of the Third Army. He provides an account of the diversionary attack on Gommecourt made July 1 to draw German forces from Beaumont Hamel. His description of the attack, a disaster, and his subsequent problems due to a wound provides a detailed picture of a peripheral effort in the offensive.

293 Hay, Ian. *Carrying On: After the First Hundred Thousand*. Edinburgh: William Blackwood and Sons, n.d. Personal account of experiences with the 9th Scottish Division from Loos through the Somme.

294 Headlam, Cuthbert. *History of the Guards Division in the Great War 1915-1918*. 2 Vols. London: John Murray, 1924. Describes the Guards in action at Flers- Courcelette and Morval and the capture of Les Boeufs. Workmanlike if prosaic account.

295 Henniker, A. M. *Transportation on the Western Front, 1914-1918*. 2 Vols. London: His Majesty's Stationery Office, 1937. Chapter VIII: "Railways in an Offensive, Neuve Chapelle and Loos--The Somme" is mostly about the Somme. The railroad situation is described at various times during 1916 to give example of problems. There would be too much detail to cover all of the construction for the offensive.

296 Henning, Hans (Baron Grote). *Somme*. Hamburg: Hanseatische Verlagsamstalt, 1937. Although skillfully written, this volume is a patchwork in which the author, whose division fought twice at the Somme, tries to show the German soldier's burdens. It would be difficult for a reader not already acquainted with the basic events of the offensive to follow Henning's account.

297 Henriques, J.Q. *The War History of the 1st Battalion Queen's Westminster Rifles*. London: Medici Society, 1923. Battalion attacked July 1 at Gommecourt suffering 600 casualties out of 750 men. It also fought at Leuze Wood and Transloy Ridges in September and October, with very heavy losses. The author says the Somme was a blow from which the Germans never recovered.

298 Hentig, Hans von. *Psychologische Strategie des Grossen Kriegs*. [Psychological Strategies of the Great War.] Heidelberg: Carl Winter, 1927. Includes experiences of fighting with the German 3rd Guard Division. Regarded the Somme as disaster for the German army and as undermining faith in the military leaders.

299 Herbert, A.P. *Secret Battle*. London: Methuen, 1919. This novel, in which the hero distinguishes himself at Gallipoli only to be shot for cowardice after the experience of the Western Front, offers a sense of the impact of the Somme offensive. It is well-written and thoughtful.

300 Herbillon, E. *Le Général Alfred Micheler D'Après ses notes, sa Correspondance et Les Souvenirs Personnels de L'Auteur*. [General Alfred Michelier From His Notes and Correspondence and the Personal Recollections of the Author.] Paris: Plon, 1933. Discussion of the Somme by one of the French commanders. Includes many of Micheler's letters giving personal impressions.

301 Herman, Gerald. *The Pivotal Conflict: A Comprehensive Chronology of the*

First World War, 1914-1919. New York: Greenwood Press, 1992. Traces events day by day with various categories, including military actions, in parallel columns. A very useful reference for organizing and establishing chronological relationships.

302   Hermann, Alfred. *Somme, Flanders, Arras.* Jena: Buchdruck Werkstälte, 1936. Hermann's unit was sent into combat three times during the Somme campaign, and he gives a vivid account of the situation from the viewpoint of a German soldier.

303   Herzfeld, Hans. *Der Erste Weltkrieg.* [The First World War.] München: Deutscher Taschenbuch Verlag, 1968. Thorough military and political history valuable for giving a sense of the German attitude about the offensive.

304   Higham, Robin, ed. *A Guide to the Sources of British Military History.* Berkeley: University of California Press, 1971. Higham has provided an excellent reference for both primary and secondary sources concerning the British military. The broad chronological coverage--prehistory to modern times-- make completeness impossible, but the book is the starting point for any research in the field.

305   Hill, Prudence. *To Know the Sky: The Life of Air Chief Marshal Sir Roderic Hill.* London: William Kimber, 1962. In 1916 Hill was with 60 Squadron of the R.F.C. which was central to the British effort of win and hold air superiority at the Somme.

306   Hills, J.D. *The Fifth Leicestershire, 1914-1918.* Loughborough: Echo Press, 1919. This unit was part of the 46th Division in the Third Army which launched the diversionary attack at Gommecourt on July 1. The diversion, though a failure, must be credited as part of the offensive.

307   Hindenburg, Generalfeldmarschall [Paul] von, *Aus meinem Leben.* Leipzig: G. Hirzel, 1920; Translation by F.A. Holt. *Out of My Life.* London: Cassell, 1920. Limited account of Somme except the decision to withdraw. "Meanwhile the situation on the Western Front had also become worse. The French and English, in very superior numbers, had hurled themselves at our relatively weak line on both sides of the Somme and pressed the defense back. Indeed, for a moment we were faced with the menace of a complete collapse."

308   *History and Memoir of the 33rd Battalion Machine Gun Corps and of the 19th, 98th, 100th and 248th M.G. Companies, Written and Illustrated by Members of the Battalion.* London: Waterlow Brothers and Layton, 1919. Describes fighting at High Wood, Delville Wood, Les Boeufs, Roncourt, Bouchavesles, and Clery with many illustrations, both paintings and

photographs. This is Graham Hutchinson's outfit and includes verbatim material from his books about firing 999,750 rounds in 12 hours at High Wood on August 23-24. Accounts of action superficial but the pictures are good.

309 Hitchcock, F.C. "Stand To": A Diary of the Trenches, 1915-18. London: Hurst and Blackett, 1937; rpt. 1988. Author was with the Leinster Regiment (24th Division) at Guillemont in summer of 1916 and provides parallel accounts by including passages from the diary of Ernst Jünger who was in German defending unit. Other action of the Leinster Regiment at the Somme is also described.

310 Hodder-Williams, R.W. Princess Patricia's Canadian Light Infantry, 1914-1919. 2 Vols. New York: Doran, 1923. This unit was badly battered in early September in the Canadian assault on Courcelette. The author's account is conventional and descriptive.

311 Hodson, J.L. Return to the Wood. London: Gollancz, 1955. The hero of this novel is disillusioned by his experiences at High Wood during the Somme offensive, becomes a pacifist, and finally must make the decision to fight Hitler. For the student of the Somme it is most valuable for its portrayal of the effect of the experience of battle on the individual.

312 Hoeppner, Ernest von. Deutschlands Krieg in der Luft. [The German War in the Air.] Leipzig: Koehler, 1921. This study of German air power is interesting from the point-of-view of the Somme because the author focuses on that battle as the nadir of the German air effort. He warmly praises the artillery spotting of the Allies, and details the German problems in 1916.

313 Hoffman, Rudolf von, ed. Der Deutsche Soldat: Briefe aus dem Weltkrieg. [The German Soldier: Letters from the World War.] München: Albert Langen-Georg Müller, 1937. Provides a number of letters describing the individual German soldiers' experience of the Somme.

314 Hopkins, John C. Canada at War, 1914-1918. New York: Doran, 1919. Hopkins provides an overall survey including domestic issues, but he includes coverage of Canadians at the front. His book is useful background.

315 Horne, Alistair. Death of a Generation: From Neuve Chapelle to Verdun and the Somme. London: MacDonald, 1970. Brief and lavishly illustrated exposition of the traditional view of 1915-16. Does conclude that the Somme cost the Germans the strategic initiative, and condemns the premature use of tanks.

316 Horne, Charles F., et al., eds. *Source Records of the Great War.* 7 Vols. N.P.:
     National Alumni, 1923. The accounts in these volumes are written by a mix
     of eyewitnesses, journalists, and historians from both sides. The chapter
     concerning the Somme is by Philip Gibbs, Prince Rupprecht of Bavaria, and
     Lieutenant Dambitsch. The approach provides balance while providing
     strongly expressed points-of-view.

317 Hughes, Colin. *Mametz: Lloyd George's Welsh Army at the Battle of the
     Somme.* Gerards Cross: Orion, 1982; rpt. 1990. Follows Lloyd George's
     efforts to create purely Welsh units and focuses on the 38th (Welsh) Division
     at Mametz Woods, July 5-12. Defends unit against Boraston's charge that its
     failure was key to the failure to break through and shows that the British
     learned quickly how to use artillery effectively after the problems of July 1.

318 Humbert, Captain. *La Division Barbot.* [The Barbot Division.] Paris: Hachette,
     1919. Provides account of the 77th Division which served in the Somme
     campaign several times.

319 Hussey, A. H., and D.S. Inman. *The Fifth Division in the Great War.* London:
     Nisbet and Co., 1921. Authors describe the experience of the 5th Division
     which attacked with two other divisions at High Wood on July 20th.
     Withdrawn August 2-3, on the 24th it moved back up to Dernancourt and
     relieved on the Eastern slopes of Maltz Horn Ridge with the French on its
     immediate right and attacked on September 3rd and 5th. After a rest, it
     attacked in the middle of the month and advanced 2 miles. September 25, it
     left the Somme for good.

320 Hutchinson, Graham Seton. *Footslogger: An Autobiography.* London:
     Hutchinson, 1931. A harrowing account of fighting at High Wood, often
     quoted and repeated by the author in other writings.

321 Hutchinson, Graham Seton. *Pilgrimage.* London: Rich and Cowan, 1935.
     Personal account of a machine gun company at High Wood. Account similar
     to author's other publications.

322 Hutchinson, Graham Seton. *The Thirty-Third Division in France and Flanders,
     1915-1919.* London: Waterlow and Sons, 1921. On the 15th the 33rd
     attacked High Wood and Martinpuich unsuccessfully, suffering from terrible
     flanking fire. On August 18th, the 33rd returned to the High Wood-Delville
     Wood area supported by Hutchinson's machine gun brigade which fired
     999,750 rounds in 12 hours. An attack on August 24 was a success and
     Delville Wood was taken. On October 28 in the Guillemont-Ginchy Ridge
     area the Division took Dewdrop Trench and attacked Hazy Trench. It also
     fought at Le Transloy, but the terrible mud resulted in little tactical gain.

Hutchinson is an eloquent but emotional critic of the offensive.

323 Hutchinson, Graham Seton. *Warrior*. London: Hutchinson, 1932. Hutchinson was in battle on July 15, 1916, as commander of a machine gun company and participated in a costly attack on Martinpuich and High Wood. He asserts that the Commander-in-Chief's staff did not agree about the Somme hence "the grandiose strategical plan never had a chance of consummation." He claims breakthrough was the real goal and pushed by Haig and Foch while Rawlinson favored series of attacks with careful preparation. A breakthrough was not impossible but lack of unity among leaders blocked chances. Gains were not exploited; reserves wasted against impregnable spots. Haig should have overruled Rawlinson and hit spots where resistance broke, for instance, up Mametz Valley to Bazentin.

324 Huxtable, Charles. *From the Somme to Singapore: A Medical Officer in Two World Wars*. Tunbridge Wells: Costello, 1988. The author was with the Warwickshires at the Somme from July 5th through the 21st and describes the unit's activities, but he provides disappointingly little information about the medical problems and issues of the struggle.

325 Impressions Gallery of Photography. *For King and Country: Battle of the Somme, 1916*. York: Impressions Gallery of Photography, 1986. Account published to accompany a traveling photo exhibition.

326 Imrie, Alex. *Pictorial History of the German Army Air Service, 1914-18*. Chicago: Henry Regnery Co., 1973. Imrie asserts that the Germans were unable to regain control of the air in 1916 despite new hunting squadrons and reinforcements with new and better fighters starting in September.

327 Inglefield, V.E. *The History of the Twentieth (Light) Division*. London: Nisbet and Co., 1921. On August 22, the 20th Division arrived on a line north of Guillemont-Montauban Road. It was to take Guillemont, and although several earlier attempts had failed, did so, with one sergeant holding with his platoon for two days without food or water. After a short rest the Division was back in action taking Morval and Les Boeufs on September 16-18 and the Brown Line overlooking Transloy on October 7. The author provides a straight forward, careful account.

328 Insall, Algernon J. *Observer's Memoirs of the R.F.C., 1915-1918*. London: William Kimber, 1970. Insall was involved with the Somme offensive at which the R.F.C. held superiority and provided useful artillery spotting.

329 Jacomt, C.E. *Torment*. London: Andrew Melrose, 1920. An account of the 2nd Division, which was engaged at Delville Wood and at Waterlot Farm in July

and August and at the Battle of the Ancre in November.

330 James, E.A. *British Regiments, 1914-1918*. London: Samson Books, 1978
     Very useful listing of the service records of British regiments during the war.

331 Jerrold, Douglas. *The Hawke Battalion: Some Personal Records of Four
     Years, 1914-1918*. London: Ernest Benn, 1925. The Battalion, part of the
     Royal Naval Division, only arrived at the Somme October 7. Jerrold did see
     action east of Thiepval, and offers a well-written account of the latter days of
     the campaign.

332 Jerrold, Douglas. *The Royal Naval Division*. London: Hutchinson and Co.,
     1923. Naval Division units were not involved at the Somme until October but
     made an attack on Beaucourt on November 13 with heavy casualties.
     Objective achieved and Division was relieved on the 15th. The author, later
     a pro-fessional historian, provides a good chapter on the battle.

333 Joffre, Joseph J. C. *Personal Memoirs*. 2 Vols. Translated by T. Bentley Mott.
     London: Bles, 1932. While certainly written to defend the author, these vol-
     umes are the only source for first hand accounts of his dealings with some
     other French officers and his account of relations with Haig and decision
     making. Blames the winter and politics for the failure on the Somme and says
     he planned to finish the job in 1917.

334 Johnson, Douglas W. *Battlefields of the World War: Western and Southern
     Fronts: A Study in Military Geography*. American Geographical Society
     Research Series, ed. by W.L.G. Joerg, No. 3. New York: Oxford University
     Press, 1921. Johnson lays out the Somme area's topography: low hills and
     valleys with heavy chalk soil. He suggests that there was good potential for
     transport and use of tanks. The area was a good choice for a breakthrough,
     although the open, rising ground over which the attackers had to move did
     provide the defenders with wide fields of fire in many places.

335 Johnson, Hubert C. *Breakthrough!: Tactics, Technology, and the Search for
     Victory on the Western Front in World War I*. Novato, CA: Presido Press,
     1994. Johnson's comments about the Somme are scattered, but given the
     importance of technology and the questions about its effective use, his book
     is very useful for the study of the offensive.

336 Johnson, J.H. *Stalemate!: The Great Trench Warfare Battles of 1915-1917*.
     London: Arms and Armour Press, 1995. Johnson's approach to the battles
     of 1915-17, including the Somme, focuses on the idea of siege warfare as he
     seeks to explain the failure of the Allies to achieve a breakthrough. He adds
     little new knowledge to the subject, however.

337   Johnston, R.E. *Ulundi to Delville Wood*. London: Simpkin Marshall, 1930.
      Biography of H.T. Lukin, who commanded the 1st South African Brigade (9th
      (Scottish) Division) which was heavily engaged at Delville Wood during the
      Somme offensive.

338   Johnstone, Tom. *Orange, Green and Khaki: The Story of the Irish Regiments
      in the Great War, 1914-18*. Dublin: Gill and Macmillan, 1992. Johnstone
      provides substantial detail about men and events with numerous quotations
      from those involved. Irish units were heavily engaged at Thiepval on July 2,
      Guillemont on September 2-4, and Ginchy on September 5-10.

339   Jones, David. *In Parenthesis*. London: Faber and Faber, 1929. Fictional
      account by a poet, who served with the 15th Royal Welsh Fusiliers, of a
      soldier's experiences culminating in being wounded at the Somme.

340   Jones, Nigel H. *The War Walk: A Journey Along the Western Front*. London:
      Robert Hale, 1983. Jones' bitterness seems fresh from the attack. Having
      noted that the bombardment failed to kill the Germans or cut the wire and this
      combined with the wave style attack doomed the effort, he remarks: "For their
      inability or unwillingness to comprehend this, and for their blindness, Haig
      and Rawlinson, respectively Commander-in-Chief and Commander of the
      Fourth Army, must be held eternally--and damningly--culpable." His account
      of the battle is relatively brief, but includes some lengthy quotes from
      participants.

341   Jones, Paul. *War Letters of a Public-School Boy*. London: Cassell, 1918.
      Although poor vision kept Jones out of combat, he served with the Army
      Service Corps and commanded an ammunition column at the Somme. His
      comments offer interesting insight into the logistical problems of the
      offensive.

342   Jones, Ralph E., George H. Rarey, and Robert J. Icks. *The Fighting Tanks Since
      1916*. Washington: National Service Publishing Co., 1933; rpt. 1969. The
      description of the fighting at the Somme in this volume is brief, but a good
      technical description of the tanks is included.

343   Jünger, Ernst. *The Storm of Steel: From the Diary of a German Storm-Troop
      Officer on the Western Front*. Translated by Basil Creighton. London: Chatto
      and Windus, 1929; orig. *In stahlgewittern*. Berlin: E.S. Mittler und Sohn,
      1922. This classic novel includes a brief but vivid account of the defense at
      Guillemont.

344   Kabisch, Ernst. *Somme, 1916*. Berlin: Otto Schlegel, 1937. Substantive account
      based on German, French, and British sources. Criticizes the French generals

for not accepting British control and the British for using tanks before they were ready. Kabisch also suggests that the German effort was hindered by personal problems between Generals Gallwitz and von Below which were only solved by giving Crown Prince Rupprecht overall command.

345   Keegan, John. *The Face of Battle*. New York: Viking Press, 1976. Keegan examined three battles: Agincourt, Waterloo, and the Somme, seeking common elements for the soldiers involved. He is a firm critic of the generalship at the Somme.

346   Keeson, C.A. Cuthbert. *The History and Records of Queen Victoria's Rifles, 1792-1922*. London: Constable, 1923. Unit fought at Gommecourt (disaster) on July 1 and in September and October at Leuze Wood, Les Boeufs, and Transloy Ridges. The strength of this account is in the inclusion of personal reminiscences.

347   Keil, Hermann. *Sächsische Reserve-Jäger-Bataillon No. 13*. [Saxon Reserve Fusilier Battalion No. 13.] Dresden: Wilhelm and Bertha von Baensch Stiftung, 1934. Includes account of defense at Longueval.

348   Kelly, D.V. *39 Months*. London: Ernest Benn, 1930. Written in 1919, the author, a captain in the 21st Division, gives an account of the bitter struggle at the Somme, particularly an encounter at Mametz Wood.

349   Kielmansegg, Peter. *Deutschland und der Erste Weltkrieg*. [Germany and the First World War.] 2 Vols. Frankfurt-au-Main: Akademisch Verlagsgeseils, 1964; 2nd ed. 1980. Description of the Somme campaign and the devastating effects of the bombardment on Germans.

350   Kiernan, Reginald H. *Captain Albert Ball: A Historical Record*. London: Hamilton, 1933. Air superiority was an important advantage for the Entente at the Somme, and Ball was one of the flyers who helped provide that edge. This biography does not, however, give much attention to the ground elements in the battle.

351   Kincaid-Smith, M. *The 25th Division in France and Flanders*. London: Harrison, 1920. The Division's involvement in the Somme campaign covered virtually the entire period and included action at Albert, Bazentin Ridge, Pozières Ridge, Mouquet Farm, and Ancre Heights.

352   Kingsford, Charles L. *The Story of the Royal Warwickshire Regiment*. London: Country Life and George Newnes, n.d. Kingsford provides brief descriptions of battalions in action at Beaumont Hamel on July 1, Montauban on July 20, and Pozières and Delville Wood on July 26.

353   Kipling, Rudyard, ed. *The Irish Guards in the Great War.* 2 Vols. London: Macmillan, 1923. Kipling's literary abilities are evident as are his sympathies. His son died with this unit. Includes accounts of the battles at Ginchy, and Les Boeufs during the Somme campaign.

354   Kirchberger, Joe H. *The First World War: An Eyewitness History.* New York: Facts on File, 1992. Provides an wealth of excerpts from firsthand accounts but lacks interpretative commentary.

355   Kitchen, Martin. *A Military History of Germany From the Eighteenth Century to the Present Day.* London: Weidenfeld and Nicolson, 1975. Although there is no discussion of the Somme battles per se in this volume, its impact which put the Germans on the strategic defensive is discussed.

356   Klein, Fritz, Willibald Gutsche, and Joachim Petzold, eds. *Deutschland im ersten Krieg.* [Germany in the First War.] 3 Vols. Berlin: Akademie-Verlag, 1968-69. Although more political than military in focus, volume two gives the Somme significant attention.

357   Knyvett, R. Hugh. *"Over There" with the Australians.* New York: Charles Scribner's Sons, 1918. Provides a first hand account of the Australians at Pozières and other battles but is unfortunately superficial in coverage.

358   Koeltz, Louis. *La Guerre de 1914-1918: les operations militaires.* [Military Operations in the War of 1914-1918.] Paris: Sirey, 1966. Military history from the French point-of-view and thus useful for understanding Joffre's intentions as well as a picture of the French share of the Somme fighting.

359   Koetzle, Hermann. *Das Sanitätswesen im Weltkrieg 1914-1918.* [Health Services in the World War 1914-18.] Stuttgart: Berger, 1924. The theme of this book is medical work with the 27th Division and the 26th Reserve Division. It has, however, some very interesting statistics concerning the high numbers of German casualties in the Somme campaign.

360   Krämer, M. *Die Geschichte des Reserve Infanterie Regiment 245 im Weltkriege, 1914-1918.* [The History of the 245th Reserve Infantry Regiment in the World War, 1914-1918.] Leipzig: Verlag Ehemalige Offiziere des R.I.R. 245, 1923. Regiment suffered almost 60% casualties between September 6 and 25 in action near Bois de Vaux.

361   Kuhl, Herman von. *Der Weltkrieg 1914-1918.* [The World War 1914-1918.] 2 Vols. Berlin: Weller, 1929. Kuhl's solid narrative includes comments about a number of elements in the Somme offensive. These include Falkenhayn's mistaken belief that the Somme was not the main thrust and

refusal, at first, to send reinforcements; British air force's spotting resulting in many German batteries being destroyed; and casualties. He notes the virtues of General Max von Gallwitz, who was brought in from Verdun to command the Second Army. He reorganized defenses and artillery, but Falkenhayn sent aid to the East and not to Gallwitz. Kuhl credits Ludendorff for building up artillery and resting worn out divisions.

362 Laffin, John. *British Butchers and Bunglers of World War One*. London: Alan Sutton, 1988. As suggested by the title, Laffin is very critical of British generals, and regards decisions by Haig and Rawlinson at the Somme as little short of murderously foolish.

363 Laffin, John, ed. *Letters From the Front, 1914-1918*. London: Dent, 1973. Laffin has included letters from both Britons and Germans with impressions of the situation during the Somme campaign.

364 Laffin, John. *A Western Front Companion, 1914-1918*. London: MBI/Alan Sutton, 1995. Laffin provides a reference for details concerning every army and battle on the Western Front including the Somme. His book is a handy and useful source for basic details.

365 Langley, Michael. *The East Surrey Regiment*. London: Leo Cooper, 1972. Good unit history with account of the regiment being devastated at Montauban on July 1.

366 Latter, J.C. *The History of the Lancashire Fusiliers*. 2 Vols. Aldershot: Gale and Polden, 1949. The accounts in these volumes follow battalions and so provide brief accounts of units in action at many of the engagements during the offensive.

367 Laure, Emile. *Les Étapes du guerre d'une division d'infanterie (13e D.I.)*. [The War Milestones of a Division of Infantry (The 13th Division of Infantry).] Paris: Berger-Levrault, 1928. The 13th Division fought at the Somme from mid-August to mid-October at Estrées-Deniécourt and Soyécourt and in November and December at Ablaincourt and Genermont.

368 Laurentin, Maurice. *Carnets d'un Fantassin 1914-1918*. [Notebooks of a Foot-Soldier 1914-1918.] N.P.: Arthaud, 1965. Organized as a daily journal, this volume provides brief but first-hand observations from the Somme front in October and November, 1916.

369 Lawson, John A. *Memories of Delville Wood: South Africa's Great Battle*. Cape Town: T. Maskew Miller, 1918. Although little more than a pamphlet, this work provides an eyewitness account of South African forces in combat.

370 Leed, Eric J. *No Man's Land: Combat and Identity in World War I*. Cambridge: Cambridge University Press, 1979. Leed's focus on the stress and other psychological effects of the trenches provides valuable context for the study of the soldiers at the Somme.

371 Lewis, Cecil. *Sagittarius Rising*. London: Peter Davies, 1936; rpt. 1969. The author was in the Royal Army Flying Corps and flew over the Somme throughout 1916. Air superiority was useful to the infantry, but Lewis' account is not particularly focused on the battle.

372 Lewis, Gwilym. *Wings Over the Somme, 1916-1918*. Edited by Chaz Bowyer. London: William Kimber, 1976. Very personal account of service in the R.F.C., and offers little about the broader issues of the campaign.

373 Lewis, R. *Over the Top with the 25th: A Chronicle of Events at Courcelette and Vimy Ridge*. Halifax: Marshall, 1918. Lewis provides a good discussion of his activities with the Canadians at Courcelette in September in this short memoir.

374 Liddell Hart, Basil H. *Foch: The Man of Orleans*. London: Eyre and Spottis-woode, 1931. Foch did not agree with the idea of the Somme attack, but prepared the plan under Joffre's order. He favored advancing only as allowed by artillery fire, while Joffre and Haig dreamed of breaking through. Foch was dubious about any major attack in 1916, and seems along, with Liddell Hart, to have regarded the repeated assaults to take a small area as "unimaginative obstinacy."

375 Liddell Hart, Basil H. *The Memoirs of Captain Liddell Hart*. 2 Vols. London: Cassell, 1965. The author, a well-known historian, is quite critical of the British plan for the Somme offensive, which he regards as inflexible and unlikely to succeed.

376 Liddell Hart, Basil H. *The Real War, 1914-1918*. Boston: Little Brown, 1930; enlarged ed. entitled *A History of the World War* (1934). Liddell Hart is critical of Haig for being inflexible and not understanding local conditions or the difficult ground which was a key to the battles. He criticizes the lack of concealment of preparation and wave formation for attack, suggesting that these resulted in losses greater than any previous force had taken and continued in action. He also regards the attacks in the fall as completely without justification.

377 Liddell Hart, Basil H. *Reputations*. London: John Murray, 1928. The shift of Liddell Hart to increasingly serious criticism of British generalship in World War I, including denouncing the rigid, unimaginative frontal assaults at the

Somme, begins with the discussion of Haig in this volume.

378   Liddell Hart, Basil H. *The Tanks: The History of the Royal Tank Regiment*. 2
      Vols. London: Cassell, 1959.   The first volume is a history of the
      development of tanks in World War I, and the author, who was involved with
      many of the personnel involved, offers useful details and comments.

379   Liddell Hart, Basil H. *Through the Fog of War*. London: Faber and Faber,
      1938. This book has a short history of the war then a series of biographical
      sketches and views of battles that include the Somme. Liddell Hart, a leading
      critic of the British high command, attacks Haig for gambling on a
      breakthrough, but notes that the general was pressured by London to
      cooperate with the French, who chose the location of the offensive. He is also
      critical of Haig for believing that the barrage would cut the wire and for not
      attacking at dawn. He suggests that the British Official History, partly due to
      political pressure, is biased in Haig's favor.

380   Liddle, Peter H. *The Airman's War 1914-18*. Poole: Bradford Press, 1987.
      Liddle provides personal accounts of flyers including some involved in the
      aggressive campaign to hold air superiority over the Somme.

381   Liddle, Peter H. *The 1916 Battle of the Somme: A Reappraisal*. London: Leo
      Cooper, 1992. In an important work of revision, Liddle rejects the usual
      criticisms of Haig and the strategic planning of the battle, and asserts that the
      Somme did indeed wear down the Germans, setting up eventual victory. He
      argues that there really was no other reasonable strategic objective and that
      the situation at Verdun made the British offensive vital. Liddle does recognize
      that there were serious problems in the offensive. Artillery support was
      inadequate due to both shortage and poor quality of shells, guns not being
      properly registered, and worn barrels. He also thinks that more could have
      been made of the July 1 gains at Montauban since the French had made
      adjacent gains, but blames Rawlinson for the decision to stop and consolidate.
      A northward move would have allowed the flanking of the Germans who were
      holding against the frontal assaults.

382   Liddle, Peter H. *The Soldier's War, 1914-1918*. London: Blandford Press,
      1988. Description of the war, including the Somme, from the point-of-view
      and often in the words of the rank and file.

383   Lindsay, J.H., ed. *The London Scottish in the Great War*. London: Regimental
      Headquarters, 1925. The First Battalion of the 56th London Division was at
      the Somme and attacked at Gommecourt on July 1. Although the unit got to
      the German trenches, it was forced to withdraw due to lack of support. It was
      involved at Leuze Wood and Angle Wood in September at east of Les Boeufs

in October. Account is clear and useful but mostly descriptive.

384   Liveing, Edward G.D. *Attack: An Infantry Subaltern's Impressions of July 1st,
      1916*. London: Heinemann, 1918; rpt. 1986. Short but effective account of
      the author's experiences as part of the 12th (London) Regiment in the initial
      attack at the Somme.

385   Livesey, Anthony. *Great Battles of World War I*. London: Marshall Editions,
      1989. Heavily illustrated popular study of the war. Pictures the Somme as
      terrible waste of British lives.

386   Lloyd, Alan. *The War in the Trenches*. London: Hart-Davis MacGibbon, 1976.
      Lloyd provides a popular, well-illustrated description of conditions in the
      trenches. He is a bit sarcastic about Haig's willingness to continue attacks in
      the face of enormous casualties and suggests that the Somme showed that
      trench warfare was becoming ever more dangerous.

387   Lloyd George, David (Earl Lloyd George of Dwyfor). *War Memoirs*. 6 Vols.
      London: Nicolson and Watson, 1933-36; numerous rpts. Although Lloyd
      George was not directly involved in the military effort, his role, along with
      Churchill, as critic of the army's focus on the Western Front as he rose to
      Prime Minister makes his comments a necessary part of studying British
      strategy. His activity as Minister of Munitions also bears on the preparations
      for the Somme.

388   Lock, Cecil Bert Lovell. *The Fighting 10th*. Adelaide: Webb and Son, 1936.
      This account of the 10th Battalion (1st Australian Division) is filled with
      biographical sketches and statistics about the men of the unit. The narrative
      account of the unit's activities including combat at Pozières is limited.

389   Lomomt, A. *Histoire de la Grande Guerre*. [History of the Great War.] Paris:
      Gedalage, 1923. An adequate survey, the author of which credits the British
      with winning the Somme by "an heroic tenacity."

390   Longmore, C. *The Old Sixteenth, Being a Record of the 16th Battalion, A.I.F.,
      During the Great War, 1914-1918*. Perth: History Committee of 16th
      Battalion, 1929. Longmore traces the 16th's involvement in the war including
      involvement at the Somme, especially at Fabeck Graben and Mouquet Farm
      in August.

391   Lossberg, Fritz von. Meine *Tätigkeit im Weltkriege 1914-1918*. [My Activity
      in the World War 1914-1918.] Berlin: E.S. Mittler und Sohn, 1939.
      Lossberg, a colonel and superior tactician, and was chief of staff to Fritz von
      Below who was brought in to command a new 1st army north of the Somme

on July 19. He began establishing defense in depth to avoid huge losses to Allied artillery--followed up by Ludendorff when he arrived.

392 Love, A.G. "Casualties and Medical Statistics of the British Forces During the World War." *Military Surgeon* 70 (Feb. 1932): 109-27. Love includes the Somme but his focus is more general.

393 Lucas, Charles, ed. *The Empire at War.* 6 Vols. London: Oxford University Press, 1921-26. Lucas divides the empire, roughly, by continents and discusses each colony's contribution to the war. He provides descriptions and comments about the activities of Australians and Canadians at the Somme.

394 Lucien-Graux, Dr. *Les Fausses Nouvelles de la Grande Guerre.* [New Falsehoods of the Great War.] 3 Vols. Paris: L'Edition Française Illustrée, 1918. Volume three has a long study called "L'offensive sur la Somme." The Somme gained little ground but from other points of view it was more satisfactory: helped with Verdun; took initiative from the Germans; disrupted the stalemate.

395 Ludendorff, Erich von. *Ludendorff's Own Story, August 1914-November 1918.* New York: Harper and Brothers, 1919. Deals with the Somme only after September 1. Speaks well of generals and privates but has little detail about the battle. The book provides perspective from the man who would soon dominate German military and government.

396 Ludendorff, Erich von. *My War Memoirs.* London: Hutchinson, 1919; 2nd ed., 2 Vols. London: Hutchinson, 1919. Ludendorff came to the Western Front during the battle, but quickly saw that the ground lost was of little consequence and that the strain on the army called for relinquishing untenable areas whereas Falkenhayn had tried to hold every inch. He used tactic of defense in depth and pushed the formation of storm trooper units. He criticizes his predecessors for being surprised by the attack. He says he did not at first realize the seriousness of the situation or he would not have sent troops to the East to deal with Rumania. He did not regard the loss of ground as serious, but much artillery was also gone and fighting power down. This is the best of Ludendorff's books for use with the Somme.

397 Lupfer, T.T. *The Dynamics of Doctrine: The Changes in German Tactical Doctrine During the First World War.* Fort Leavenworth, KS: Command and General Staff College, 1981. An interesting analysis that provides insight into the German defensive schemes at the Somme.

398 Luxford, J.H. *With the Machine Gunners in France and Palestine: Being the Official History of the New Zealand Machine Gun Corps.* Auckland:

Whitcombe and Tombs, 1923. Provides a detailed account of the Corps at the Battle of Flers-Courcelette (September 15) and then through early October. The account is unfortunately lacking in context.

399   Lyttelton, Oliver (Viscount Chandos). *The Memoirs of Lord Chandos.* New York: New American Library, 1963. The author served in the Guards Division, and gives a detailed but quite personal account of combat at Flers and Les Boeufs.

400   McBride, Herbert W. *A Rifleman Went to War.* Marines, N.C: Small Arms Press, 1935; rpt. 1987. Author was with the 21st Battalion of the Canadian Expeditionary Force. The focus of the book is on weapons, especially the rifle, but there is an account of the fighting at the Somme.

401   McBride, H.W. *The Emma Gees.* [Machine Guns.] Indianapolis: Bobs-Merrill, 1918; rpt. 1988. This memoir is by an American who served with the Canadian Expeditionary Force. Although he won a medal in 1916 his account of that year is unfortunately cursory.

402   McCarthy, Chris. *The Somme: The Day-by-Day Account.* London: Arms and Armour Press, 1993. McCarthy has compiled an enormously detailed account of the offensive quite literally day-by-day and unit-by-unit. This is an extremely valuable reference work.

403   McClintock, A. *Best o' Luck.* Toronto: McClelland, Goodchild and Stewart, 1917. Detailed memoir by an American serving with the 87th Battalion of the Canadian Expeditionary Force.

404   MacDonagh, Michael. *The Irish on the Somme.* London: Hodder and Stoughton, 1917. Provides a popular account of the experiences of Irish units, especially the Ulster Division, which won much praise for its attack near Thiepval on July 1. Volume published in the U.S. as *The Irish at the Front.*

405   MacDonald, Lyn. *The Roses of No Man's Land.* London: Michael Joseph, 1980. This account of the British nursing services offers significant insight into the casualty figures of the Somme campaign and the suffering of the wounded.

406   MacDonald, Lyn. *Somme.* London: Michael Joseph, 1983. MacDonald makes very effective use of oral sources and unpublished diaries to give a real sense of the everyday British soldier's experience. She tends to defend the British command and to blame inadequate communications technology rather than Haig or other commanders for the failure to break off hopeless situations during the attack. Unlike many other historians, MacDonald praises the

accuracy of British artillery fire due to the R.F.C. and the good photos taken, citing German references in support. She notes political elements in decisions about final attacks in November. Haig wanted "trumps" in dealing with French pressure to keep the Germans busy and to get the politicians to agree to 350,000 reinforcements for 1917--got enough cards for both goals, despite the limited successes in taking Beaumont Hamel and other fighting in November.

407   McEntee, Girard L. *Military History of the World War*. New York: Charles Scribner's Sons, 1937. Outline history heavily illustrated with maps.

408   MacGill, P. *The Great Push*. London: Herbert Jenkins, 1916. Concerns the 47th Division, which was in action at High Wood in September. The account is superficial, however.

409   MacGill, Patrick. *The Diggers, the Australians in France*. London: Herbert Jenkins, 1919. Brief account of the Australian forces on the Western Front.

410   McGuinness, Frank. *Observe the Sons of Ulster Marching Toward the Somme*. London: Faber and Faber, 1986. McGuinness's play climaxes with the attack of the 36th (Ulster) Division on July 1. It is an expression of nationalist Protestant Irish sentiment about union with England and Irish sacrifice for the country.

411   MacIntosh, J.C. *Men and Tanks*. London: John Lane, The Bodley Head, 1920. MacIntosh's description of life and combat in the earliest tanks is detailed and interesting. Unfortunately, he fails to tie his observations to the events of the offensive; the battle described is, however, apparently Flers.

412   Mackenzie, K.W. *The Story of the Seventeenth Battalion, A.I.F. in the Great War, 1914-1918*. Sydney: Shipping Newspapers, 1946. Provides account of the Battalion, which was in action at Pozières and Mouquet Farm in July and August.

413   MacKesy, J.P. "The Battle of the Somme: R.E. Preparations in the 31st Divisional Area." *Royal Engineers' Journal* (Dec. 1919): 275-8. Brief examination of one division's part of the enormous effort to prepare for battle.

414   MacKesy, Kenneth. *Tank Warfare: A History of Tanks in Battle*. New York: Stein and Day, 1972. Brief account of tank action at the Somme.

415   Macmillan, Harold. *Winds of Change*. New York: Harper, 1966. The future Prime Minister provides a short account of combat and being wounded with the 2nd Battalion of the Grenadier Guards near Ginchy in mid-September,

1916. He provides insight into the impact of the war on the future rulers of Great Britain.

416 MacPhail, Andrew. *Official History of the Canadian Forces in the Great War: The Medical Services*. Ottawa: The King's Printer, 1923. Somme was the first heavy action for all four Canadian divisions. The first three were in the line from September 3 to October 16, and the fourth from October 17 to November 28. Canadian front was about 3,000 yards and casualties so heavy that the medical units were pooled to deal with the situation. MacPhail provides a detailed narrative.

417 McPherson, William L. *A Short History of the Great War*. New York: G.P. Putnam's Sons, 1920. Descriptive history but with the suggestion that the Somme did pay off.

418 McPherson, William L. *The Strategy of the Great War*. New York: G.P. Putnam's Sons, 1919. The Somme was the supreme effort to regain a war of movement, but the original strategic goals have been brushed under the carpet because things did not go well. The Somme paid off in 1917-18, the first sign being German withdrawal to the Hindenburg Line early in 1917. McPherson notes that Haig's rather limited goals about relieving Verdun, helping keep German forces from moving to the East, and wearing down the Germans, but thinks there were greater goals too.

419 Maddocks, Graham. *The Liverpool Pals: The 17th, 18th, 19th, and 20th (Service) Battalions The King's (Liverpool) Regiment*. London: Leo Cooper, 1991. Thorough account of these battalions, which were part of the 89th Brigade, 30th Division, and helped to take Montauban on July 1. They saw further action in July and in October.

420 Magnus, Laurie. *The West Riding Territorials in the Great War*. London: Kegan Paul, Trench, Trubner and Co., 1920. Unit fought in the Thiepval Wood area from beginning of battle until mid-September. Magnus is quite critical of reports from larger units that fail to acknowledge his battalion's sacrifice. He also notes that labor requirements for logistical preparation interfered with training.

421 Malins, Geoffrey H. *How I Filmed the War*. New York: Stokes, 1919; rpt. 1993. Malins made the very popular, though partially staged, 1916 film of action at the Somme. His book, however, is a description of what he saw at the front as he was taking pictures, and provides many details.

422 Mangin, E. *Lettres de Guerre, 1914-1918*. [War Letters, 1914-1918.] Paris: Librairie Arthème Fayard, 1950. The letters included in this volume give

more attention to Verdun than the Somme, but discussion of the overall situation is included.

423   Mangin, E. *Un Regiment Lorrain: Le 79e Verdun-La Somme.* [A Regiment of Lorraine: The 79th at Verdun and the Somme.] Paris: Payot, 1934. The author was commander of the 79th Regiment of the 11th Division of XX Corps from September, 1914, through July, 1916, and fought at Verdun and the Somme. His account of tactics suggests that there was little difference between the British and French despite the latter's greater success.

424   Manning, Frederic. *The Middle Parts of Fortune: Somme and Ancre, 1916.* London: Peter Davies, 1977.   This autobiographical novel has been published in several forms. Initially it appeared privately, then in 1930 as *Her Privates, We* by Private 19022, and finally in full in 1977. The story is entirely set in the period of the Somme offensive and at the front. It offers an excellent sense of the trials and tribulations of the typical private soldier.

425   Marden, T.O. *A Short History of the Sixth Division August 1914-March 1919.* London: Hugh Rees, 1920. Very brief account of the Division which joined the 5th Army at end of July and spent most of August on the Ancre opposite Beaumont-Hamel. September 6-8, shifted to XIV Corps in the 4th Army and went to Ginchy and Leuze Wood for attack on the Quadrilateral which was made September 12-15 but failed. Had more success on the 25th near Morval. Remained in line until October 20.

426   Mark VII [Max Plowman.] *A Subaltern on the Somme.* London: Dent, 1927; many rpts. A good account of life behind the lines and in support trenches but offers little account of actual combat.

427   Marshall, S.L.A. *The American Heritage History of World War I.* New York: American Heritage, 1964; rpt. 1987. Solid survey which sets the Somme experience effectively into context and written by one of the leading military historians of the current era.

428   Marshall-Cornwall, James. *Foch as Military Commander.* New York: Crane, Russak and Co., 1972. Notes that Foch did not particularly like the choice of the Somme for attack but took orders when Joffre insisted. The battle had no meaningful strategic rationale other than wearing down the Germans, which given the defenses was not logical. Comments that failure to reinforce success in the south was lost opportunity and that after failure of July 15 the battle should have been broken off. Foch was unfairly blamed.

429   Marshall-Cornwall, James. *Haig as Military Commander.* London: Batsford, 1973. The author, a junior officer at Haig's headquarters in 1916-17, regards

charges that Haig was unimaginative and brutal as misunderstandings. He supports the concept that the battle was to wear down the German forces and suggests that despite mistakes, tanks were appropriately used. He cites Duff Cooper and John Terraine as best biographers of Haig. He criticizes Haig's choice of subordinates, however, and thinks that he was overly expectant of a breakthrough.

430   Martel, G. Le Q. *In the Wake of the Tank: The First Fifteen Years of Mechanization in the British Army.* London: Sifton Praed and Co., 1931. Martel's description of 1916 is brief, but he does support the argument that tanks were prematurely used.

431   Martin, Bernard. *Poor Bloody Infantry: A Subaltern on the Western Front, 1916-1917.* London: John Murray, 1987. Martin includes a brief account of an attack at Guillemont in September, but his memoir is mostly useful for its picture of the condition and attitude of troops behind the lines during the offensive.

432   Martin, Christopher. *Battle of the Somme.* London: Wayland, 1973. Brief summary of the campaign mostly for students, but well grounded in published eyewitness accounts.

433   Masefield, John. *The Battle of the Somme.* London: Heinemann, 1919. A useful, well-written survey focused on the rank and file, but limited by the author's limited sources of information.

434   Masefield, John. *The Old Front Line.* London: Heinemann, 1917. Topology was a key to the battles of the Somme, and Masefield's lyrical description of the area gives a sense of what soldiers faced.

435   Maude, Alan H., ed. *The 47th (London) Division.* London: Amalgamated Press, 1922. Maude provides a descriptive account of a division in combat. September 10-12 it replaced the First Division in High Wood area. It attacked on September 15th, and after rough going (tanks could not get over the ground) High Wood was cleared. It then had mixed success till relieved on the 19th, and was then part of a renewed attack on the Flers line later in the month and out of the Somme for good October 9. The volume includes some account of support services.

436   Maurice, Frederick. *British Strategy.* London: Constable, 1929. Maurice, a British general, provides an analysis of strategy concluding that "wearing down" was crude generalship and to be used only as a last resort.

437   Maurice, Frederick. *Lessons of Allied Co-operation: Naval, Military and Air*

1914-1918. London: Oxford University Press, 1942. Maurice's analysis arises from the perspective of the beginning of World War II. He notes that despite the collapse of France (1940) lessons about cooperation from World War I have been learned. Haig's orders when he took command stressed cooperation with France. The book is heavily based on the official histories but offers an unusual focus.

438 Maurice, Frederick. *Life of General Lord Rawlinson of Trent.* London: Cassell, 1928. A rather overly friendly study of the general who commanded the main attacking army at the Somme.

439 Maurice, Frederick. *The 16th Foot: A History of the Bedfordshire and Hertfordshire Regiment.* London: Constable, 1931. Although this is a good history, the single volume format makes for sketchy coverage.

440 Maxwell, Frank. *Frank Maxwell, VC.* London: John Murray, 1921. Maxwell, who was killed in 1917, commanded the 12th Battalion of the Middlesex Regiment in the 18th Division at the Somme. He was at Montauban and wrote to his wife describing the situation and complaining that an opportunity to push cavalry into open country had been wasted.

441 Mayer, S.L., and W.J. Koenig. *The Two World Wars: A Guide to the Manuscript Collections in the United Kingdom.* London: Bowker, 1976. Despite some gaps this is an excellent reference for manuscript sources held by museums and archives, large and small, public and private.

442 Maze, Paul. *A Frenchman in Khaki.* London: Heinemann, 1934. Author was liaison attached to General Hubert Gough and was sent to observe various aspects of the Somme campaign. His accounts are articulate and detailed.

443 Mead, Peter. *The Eye in the Air: History of Air Observation and Reconnaissance for the Army 1785-1945.* London: Her Majesty's Stationery Office, 1983. Mead includes a solid chapter about the Somme, discussing the importance of spotting for the artillery and noting that the Somme was the first example of combined air-ground arms in battle.

444 Mellersh, H.E.L. *Schoolboy Into War.* London: William Kimber, 1978. Young officer learns about war at the Somme and Passchendaele.

445 Members of the Battalion. *Scrapbook of the 7th Bn. Somerset Light Infantry.* Alesbury: Kingsbury Press, n.d. The value of this rather slim book arises from the inclusion of first hand accounts which include two focused on Guillemont and one on Les Boeufs.

446   Messenger, Charles. *Trench Fighting 1914-1918*. New York: Ballantine Books, 1972. This volume is a well illustrated survey of the Western Front with a useful description of the action at the Somme. It is a good introduction to the situation.

447   Michelin. *Les Batailles de la Somme*. Clermont-Ferrand: Michelin, 1920. Traveler's guide to the battlefield.

448   Middlebrook, Martin. *The First Day on the Somme*. London: Allen Lane, 1971. In an excellent account of the initial phase of the battle, Middlebrook discusses both strategy and tactics. Although critical of the latter and regretful that the Somme doomed what he regards as real hints of German willingness to compromise, he ultimately concludes that there was no practical alternative to the battle. Middlebrook largely absolves Haig from fault, suggesting that plans for breakthroughs and such were really contingency plans--good to be ready if everything went particularly well. He blames Rawlinson, commander of the 4th Army, who: insisted on methodical wave formation and attack at a walk rather than rushes by small groups; insisted on long, i.e., five-day, bombardment (Haig suggested but did not order shorter time to avoid warning foe) and no rolling barrage to protect troops; failed to exploit success on the British right even when Congreve reported from Montauban that he was through all lines of defense. The overall result was a longer, bloodier battle with little result for the effort. Middlebrook, unlike a number of other historians, does give the British artillery good marks for counter-battery fire based on spotting from the R.F.C., which controlled the air.

449   Mielke, Frederick. "1916: The Crisis of World War I." *Military Review* 67 (May 1987): 70-79. Discussion of trench war and casualties including the Somme.

450   Mitchell, F. *Tank Warfare: The Story of Tanks in the Great War*. London: Thomas Nelson and Sons, 1933. Chapter 3 concerns the Somme--notes high command in France insisted on using tanks over cautions of Imperial General Staff and the French. Mitchell describes various successes and failures, German fear, and Tommy's amusement. He comments about what could have been accomplished later with more and better machines, but asserts that promise of the machine was recognized.

451   Mitchell, George Deane. *Backs to the Wall*. Sydney: Angus and Robertson, 1937. Account of the 48th Battalion, 4th Australian Division in action in early August near Courcelette.

452   Mitchell, T.J., and G.M. Smith. *Casualties and Medical Statistics of the Great War: Official Medical History of the War*. London: His Majesty's Stationery

Office, 1931. This is a useful collection of information, but John Terraine argues forcefully that the casualty numbers are not reliable.

453   Molesworth, G. N., ed. *A Soldier's War: Being the Diary of the Late Arthur Henry Cook, D.C.M., M.M., B.E.M., Written during Four Years' service with the 1st Battalion, The Somerset Light Infantry, on the Western Front, France, during the Great War, 1914-18.* Taunton: E. Goodman and Son, n.d. Cook's unit fought at the Somme on July 1 on Redan Ridge near Beaumont Hamel. Casualties were so high that it was moved to a supporting role for the rest of the year.

454   Moody, R.S.H. *Historical Records of the Buffs East Kent Regiment (3rd Foot) Formerly Designated the Holland Regiment and Prince George of Denmark's Regiment 1914-1919.* London: Medici Society, 1923. Moody provides descriptions of the regiment's four battalions at various parts of the Somme, including Albert, Pozières, Transloy, Thiepval, Delville Wood, Flers-Courcelette, and Morval.

455   Moran, Lord. *The Anatomy of Courage.* London: Constable, 1945; new ed. 1966. Moran's interest is really the psychology of men in the stress of combat, but he devotes a chapter specifically to the Somme as illustrative of his theories.

456   Mordacq, J.J.H. *Les légendes de la Grande Guerre.* [Stories of the Great War.] Paris: Flammarion, 1935. Mordacq suggests that gains of the colonial corps units in the French part of the offensive should have been followed up, and asserts that significant success could have been achieved had that been done.

457   Morrow, John H., Jr. *The Great War in the Air: Military Aviation From 1909 to 1921.* Washington: Smithsonian Institution Press, 1993. Morrow provides an interesting account of the air forces of both sides in the war. His discussion includes Allied air superiority at the Somme, but his focus is more on technology and pilots than the battle.

458   Mortane, Jacques. *Guynemer, the Ace of Aces.* Translated by Clifton Harby Levy. New York: Moffat, Yard and Co., 1918. Mortane provides a good study of the air war from the French point-of-view. Guynemer was one of the Entente flyers who won and held air superiority over the Somme.

459   Morton, Desmond, and J.L. Granatstein. *Marching to Armageddon: Canadians and the Great War 1914-1919.* Toronto: Lester and Orpen Dennys, 1989. These authors provide a brief survey of Canadian activity at the Somme, which began early in September. They are critical of Haig for continuing to attack despite inclement weather late in the fall and assert that casualties were

roughly equal for the two sides. The book is a useful introduction to Canadian activity in the offensive.

460 Moser, Otto von. *Die Württemberger in Weltkrieg.* [Wurtembergers in the World War.] Stuttgart: Belser, 1928. History of the Wurttemberg divisions, a number of which spent long periods at the Somme. Unfortunately, Moser fails to give casualty figures for these units.

461 Moser, Otto von. *Kürzer strategischer überblick über den Weltkrieg.* [A Brief Study of World War Strategy.] Berlin: E.S. Mittler und Sohn, 1921. The theme of the book is strategy, and the author discusses the Somme in that context. He asserts that the Germans paid a terrible price in blood and morale and consequently lost the strategic initiative on the most important front in 1916.

462 Mottram, R.H., John Easton, and Eric Partridge. *Three Personal Records of the War.* London: Scholartis Press, 1929. Both Mottram, the author of the Spanish Farm Trilogy which includes a book about the Somme, and Partridge, who was with the Australian infantry, include some description of the battle. The accounts are episodic and not set in context of the overall situation.

463 Moyer, Laurence V. *Victory Must Be Ours: Germany in the Great War, 1914-1918.* New York: Hippocrene, 1995. Moyer provides an valuable addition to our knowledge of German efforts in World War I, particularly because his work is in English. Unfortunately he gives limited attention to the military aspects of the Somme.

464 Moynihan, Michael, ed. *People at War, 1914-1918.* Newton Abbot: David and Charles, 1973. Collection of war stories from Imperial War Museum collection supplemented by responses to request in Sunday Times. Chapter about the Somme lacks context in which to set the personal details given.

465 Munby, J.E., ed. *A History of the 38th (Welsh) Division.* London: Hugh Rees, 1920. Very slim book describing the role of the Division, which arrived at Mametz on July 5 and was to take Mametz Wood. On July 10th it made a full attack. Savage fighting followed, but by afternoon of the 11th the wood was cleared and the Division was relieved. Mametz was the largest wood taken in the Somme battles.

466 Murphy, C.C.R. *The History of the Suffolk Regiment 1914-1927.* London: Hutchinson, 1928. Six of the regiment's battalions were at the Somme and involved during the entire campaign. Accounts here are quite short but useful for details of the individual units.

467 Nasmith, G.C. *Canada's Sons and Great Britain in the World War.* Toronto: John Winston, 1919. Nasmith hoped to give Canadians a sense of their contribution to the war, including the fighting. His book is a complete survey of Canadian involvement.

468 Neuburg, Victor. *A Guide to the Western Front: A Companion for Travellers.* London: Penguin, 1988. Although actually intended for modern tourists, this guide provides good maps and descriptions of the places where important engagements occurred. It also does an effective job of noting the action that occurred at each location.

469 Neumann, Georg P. *Die Deutschen Luftstreitkräfte im Weltkriege.* Berlin: E.S. Mittler und Sohn, 1920; Translated by J.E. Gurdon as *The German Airforce in the Great War.* London: Hodder and Stoughton, 1920. Includes an account of the German effort to counter Anglo-French air superiority over the Somme and comments from German infantrymen about the incompetence of their air arm.

470 Newton, L.M. *The Story of the Twelfth: A Record of the 12th Battalion, A.I.F. During the Great War of 1914-1918.* Hobart: J. Walch and Sons for the 12th Battalion Association, 1925. Newton describe the Battalion in action especially at Pozières and Mouquet Farm. His account is detailed but mostly descriptive.

471 Nicholls, Jonathan. *Cheerful Sacrifice: The Battle of Arras, 1917.* London: Leo Cooper, 1980. Nicholls' contribution to the understanding of the Somme is indirect. His description of the British success at Arras includes a comparison with the Somme showing how much British generalship and tactical skill had improved.

472 Nichols, G.H.F. *The 18th Division in the Great War.* Edinburgh: William Blackwood and Sons, 1922. This well written volume provides details of the involvement of the Division's battalions at a number of Somme engagements: Albert, Bazentin Ridge, Trônes Woods, Delville Wood, Thiepval Ridge, Schwaben Redoubt.

473 Nicolson, G.W.L. *The Fighting Newfoundlanders: A History of the Royal Newfoundland Regiment.* St. Johns: Government of Newfoundland, 1964. Nicolson provides a solid but mostly descriptive narrative of the Regiment's attack (as part of the 29th Division) on Beaumont Hamel, July 1. Casualties were so severe in the unsuccessful effort that the regiment was withdrawn from the offensive, returning only in October to make a much more successful attack at Gueudecourt.

474   Nicolson, G.W.L. *Official History of the Canadian Army in the First World War: Canadian Expeditionary Force, 1914-1918*. Ottawa: Queen's Printer, 1962. Useful for details of the Canadian effort at the Somme. The Canadian divisions were engaged starting with the September 15th attacks.

475   Nicholson, W.N. *Behind the Lines*. London: Jonathan Cape, 1939. Unusual view of staff work in support of the 51st Division. Suggests that the frequent disdain for the rear echelon is inappropriate.

476   Noffsinger, James Philip. *World War I Aviation Books in English: An Annotated Bibliography*. Metuchen, N.J.: Scarecrow Press, 1987. Not all entries in this bibliography of 1663 items are annotated and neither annotations nor index provides much help for those seeking to study the interrelationship of air and ground fighting.

477   Norman, Aaron. *The Great Air War*. London: Collier, Macmillan, 1968. Although information about the Somme is scattered in the volume, there is a chapter on 1916 and discussion of the short-term allied air superiority during the campaign.

478   Norman, Terry. *The Hell They Called High Wood*. London: William Kimber, 1984. An excellent and detailed account of the struggle to take High Wood--one of the most bitterly contested battles of the Somme offensive.

479   [Norris, A.] *Mainly for Mother*. Toronto: Ryerson Press, 1920. Norris, a young Canadian private in 1916, provides an account of going over the top during the Somme battles, possibly at Courcelette in September.

480   Norris, Geoffrey. *The Royal Flying Corps: A History*. London: Frederick Muller, 1965. Norris provides a solid history of the R.F.C. which provided the British air superiority over the Somme thus protecting their preparations from direct observation and did important spotting work for the artillery.

481   Oatts, L.B. *Proud Heritage: The Story of the Highland Light Infantry*. 3 Vols. London: Thomas Nelson--Vols. 1 and 2; Glasgow: Grant--Vol. 3, 1952-61. Provides account of Highlanders in action during a number of the battles in July including Albert, High Wood, Ovillers, Delville Wood and Martinpuich.

482   O'Connor, V. C. Scott. *The Scene of War*. Edinburgh: William Blackwood and Sons, 1917. Writer visited many of the theaters of the war including France in 1916. His account of the Somme is lacking in details and offers little of significance.

483   Oman, Charles. "The German Losses on the Somme." *The Nineteenth Century*

and After 101 (May 1927): 694-705. Oman asserts that the casualty figures in Winston Churchill's World Crisis showing that the British and French lost twice as many men as the Germans during the offensive are wrong. He seeks to make a case that the casualties were roughly even at just under a half million for each side.

484   Ommaney, C.H. *The War History of the 1st Northumbrian Brigade R.F.A. (T.F.).* Newcastle: Hinson, 1927. Accounts of artillery are relatively rare making this a worthwhile contribution although the 50th Division, of which this Brigade was a part, involved only briefly at the Somme: Flers-Courcelette and Morval in September and Transloy Ridges in October.

485   O'Neil, H.C. *The Royal Fusiliers in the Great War.* London: Heinemann, 1922. Battalions of the Royal Fusiliers served with several divisions in action at the Somme making it difficult to give a cohesive account of the overall unit. O'Neil does manage to write a readable description, however.

486   Orgill, Douglas. *The Tank: Studies in the Development and Use of a Weapon.* London: Heinemann, 1970. Orgill provides a good introduction to early tank warfare. He defends the decision to use tanks at the Somme and credits Haig with being interested in the weapon by the end of 1915.

487   Orr, Philip. *The Road to the Somme: Men of the Ulster Division Tell their Story.* Belfast: Blackstaff, 1987. Orr questions the idea that the Ulster force was motivated by political and religious zeal, and suggests that their achievements at Thiepval on July 1 were due to innovative tactics. They moved out into no man's land before the barrage ended. This is a particularly well done divisional history.

488   "'The Other Side of the Hill' No. I: The German Defense During the Battle of the Somme, July, 1916, Derived from German Sources of Information." *Army Quarterly* 7 (Oct., 1923-Jan. 1924): 245-59. Overview of the struggle from the German perspective.

489   "'The Other Side of the Hill' No. II: The German Defense During the Battle of the Somme, July, 1916, Derived from German Sources." *The Army Quarterly* 8 (April-July 1924): 72-85. Discusses German defensive efforts at Thiepval and Beaumont Hamel. Good picture of the German efforts to rally, reinforce, and counter-attack.

490   "'The Other Side of the Hill' No. IV: Mametz Wood and Contalmaison, 9th-10th July, 1916." *Army Quarterly* 9 (Oct. 1924-Jan. 1925): 245-59. Account of the German defense in English based on German sources. Provides useful details of unsuccessful defensive efforts.

491 "'The Other Side of the Hill' No. V: Delville Wood, 14th-19th, July, 1916." *Army Quarterly* 10 (April-July 1925): 58-69. Defenders' reorganization in response to attack, loss of the wood on July 15, and counter-attack on the 19th are all described.

492 "'The Other Side of the Hill' No. VI: The German Defense of Bernafay and Trônes Woods: 2nd-14th July, 1916." *Army Quarterly* 13 (Oct. 1926-Jan. 1927): pt. 1--19-32; pt. 2--252-60. Continuation of the series discussing the Germans defensive efforts at a number of the battles of the Somme.

493 "'The Other Side of the Hill' No. IX: The Somme: 15th of September, 1916." *Army Quarterly* 26 (April-Sept. 1933): 300-08. Examines the situation of German divisions hit by the renewed British offensive of mid-September.

494 "'The Other Side of the Hill' No. X: The Capture of Thiepval, 26 September 1916." *Army Quarterly* 27 (Oct. 1933-Jan. 1934): 215-24. Describes the reactions of the German units attempting to defend Thiepval against the renewed British attack of mid-September.

495 "'The Other Side of the Hill' No. XI: In Front of Beaumont-Hamel: 13th of November, 1916." *Army Quarterly* 28 (April-July 1934): 27-36. Account of the German experience of the final battle of the Somme. Unlike the earlier essays in this series, no references are provided.

496 Otto, Helmut, Karl Schmiedel, and Helmut Schnitter, *Der erste Weltkrieg.* [The First World War.] Berlin: Beutscher Militärverlag, 1968. Solid German military history with full account of the Somme. Unlike some English sources the authors say that Allied casualties were significantly greater than German.

497 Palat, B.E. [Pierre Lehautcourt.] *La Grande Guerre sur le front occidental.* [The Western Front in the Great War.] 15 Vols. Paris: Berger-Levrault, 1917-30). Palat's work is as thorough and detailed but much more readable than the French Official History. Volume 11 concerns the Somme. Palat suggests Joffre did not expect a breakthrough but Haig did. He credits Haig with the accord between the Allies and blames the failure on inexperience, ineffective bombardment, and mud. He is not always dependable for details about the British.

498 Palat, B.E. [Pierre Lehautcourt.] *La part de Foch dan la Victoire.* [Foch's Role in the Victory.] Paris: Charles-Lavauzelle, 1930. Solid chapter about the Somme and Foch.

499 Palmer, Frederick. *With the New Army on the Somme: My Second Year of the War.* London: John Murray, 1917. An admiring and largely superficial

account of the British effort by an American correspondent.

500   Panichas, G.A., ed. *Promise of Greatness: The War of 1914-1918*. London:
      Cassell, 1968. This collection of essays honoring the fiftieth anniversary of
      the end of the war includes comment about the Somme, but the lack of an
      index makes selective reading in the volume difficult.

501   Parker, Ernest. *Into Battle 1914-1918*. London: Longmans, 1964. Parker's brief
      memoir of service with the 10th Durham Light Infantry includes a harrowing
      account of an attack in mid-September from Delville Wood toward Gueude-
      court. After his battalion suffered horrible casualties, Parker was stranded
      several hundred yards in front of the British line for a day and night. His
      description is an interesting account from a private's perspective.

502   Pearse, H.W. and H.S. Sloman. *History of the East Surrey Regiment*. 2 Vols.
      London: Medici Society, 1924. Battalions of the East Surrey Regiment
      served with a number of divisions at various times and places during the
      Somme campaign. This is a workmanlike effort but handicapped by covering
      eighteen battalions.

503   Petre, F. Lorraine. *The History of the Norfolk Regiment, 1685-1918*. 2 Vols.
      Norwich: Jarrold and Sons, [1924.] Provides accounts of five battalions in
      combat during the Somme campaign. Accounts are quite brief but do offer
      some details of the action.

504   Petre, F. Lorraine, Wilfrid Ewart, and Cecil Lowther. *The Scots Guards in the
      Great War, 1914-1918*. London: John Murray, 1925. Although initially part
      of the reserve force, in September the Division fought at Ginchy and Les
      Boeufs with heavy casualties but taking its objectives. Volume has
      reasonable account of action.

505   Pierrefeu, Jean de. *G.Q.G. Secteur 1*. 2 Vols. Paris: L'Édition Française Illustre,
      1920; Translated by C.J.C. Street as *French Headquarters, 1915-1918*.
      London: Bles, 1924. The focus is command level but the book does provide
      a description of the Somme's importance for relief of Verdun and discussion
      of French methods. Good for comparison with the British.

506   Pimienta, Robert. *La Belle épopée de l'alsacienne, 1914-1919*. [The Glorious
      Epic of the Alsatians.] 2 Vols. Paris: Peyronnet, 1932. Effective account of
      a French unit at Bois de Hein in August and September, near Sailly-Saillisel
      in October, and Metzeral in late November.

507   Poincaré, Raymond. *Au service de la France*. 7 Vols. Paris: Plon, 1926-33;
      Translated by George Arthur as *The Memoirs of Raymond Poincaré*. New

York: Doubleday and Doran, 1931. Vital to the study of French politics since a summary of Cabinet meetings is included and no official minutes were kept.

508   Pollard, A.F. *A Short History of the Great War*. London: Methuen, 1920. Unusually well-written volume by a very good historian. The author provides much critical comment along with the narrative.

509   Ponsonby, Frederick. *The Grenadier Guards in the Great War of 1914-1918*. 3 Vols. London: Macmillan, 1920. Accounts organized by battalion. First and fourth were at the Somme in September and made successful attacks, particularly at Les Boeufs.

510   Pound, Reginald. *The Lost Generation*. London: Constable, 1964. Pound argues that the volunteer tradition took the best and brightest of the British into the war, and in the battles of the Somme offensive they were decimated.

511   Priestley, R.E. *The Signal Service in the European War of 1914 to 1918 (France)*. Chatham: Mackay, 1921. Part of the official history of the Royal Engineering Corps, this volume provides important background on the problems of communications that dogged every operation on the Western Front.

512   Prior, Robin. *Churchill's 'World Crisis' as History*. London: Croom Helm, 1983. Provides useful summaries of the disputes concerning comparison of British and German casualties and the use of tanks at the Somme. Prior argues that Churchill was probably right in asserting that the British had significantly more casualties than the Germans and wrong in his attack on the use of tanks. Haig's decision to use tanks, however, was based on equally erroneous ideas and was right by luck.

513   Prior, Robin and Trevor Wilson. *Command on the Western Front: The Military Career of Sir Henry Rawlinson, 1914-18*. Oxford: Basil Blackwell, 1992. An excellent study of strategic and tactical planning and operations in World War I. Although often critical of Rawlinson, the authors argue that he was more innovative than Haig, but was forced to accept Haig's plans due to political obligation as well as taking orders from a superior. Both of the commanders were, however, very slow to learn from the experience of combat.

514   Prior, Robin, and Trevor Wilson. "15 September 1916: The Dawn of the Tank." *Journal of the Royal United Service Institution* 136 (Autumn 1991): 61-65. Discusses use of tanks at Flers-Courcelette and suggests that problems were more due to poor use of artillery than to the tanks.

515   Puleston, William D. *High Command in the World War*. New York: Charles
      Scribner's Sons, 1934. The author, a naval officer, tries to analyze the failures
      of World War I, and takes a Westerner's attitude. He comments on
      Falkenhayn's disgrace during the Somme in which the British "pounded" the
      Germans. His book does not live up to its title, for it is really mostly a des-
      criptive history.

516   Purdom, Charles B., ed. *Everyman at War: Sixty Personal Narratives of the
      War*. London: Dent, 1930. Contains two accounts of the Somme: Fred Bull,
      who was drunk and missed the initial attack but fought later with the
      Manchester Pals, and S. J. Worsley, who was in the terrible struggle at
      Delville Wood.

517   Puyperoux, Général. *La 3e division coloniale dans la Grande Guerre*. [The 3rd
      Colonial Division in the Great War.] Paris: Fournier, 1919. Account of unit
      involved in the initial attack in July and which returned to action in August.

518   Raimes, A.L. *The Fifth Battalion The Durham Light Infantry 1914-1918*. N.P.:
      By a Committee of Past and Present Officers of the Battalion, 1931. This
      Battalion attacked at High Wood Ridges on September 15, and took its
      objective at the price of very high casualties. Then on September 25-28 it
      was in the advance to the Flers line and October 23 fought at Butte de
      Warlencourt, beyond the Flers Line remaining in action into November.

519   Raleigh, Walter, and H.A. Jones. *History of the Great War Based on Official
      Documents: The War in the Air*. 6 Vols. Oxford: Clarendon Press, 1922-37.
      The Somme offensive, at which the British held air superiority, is described
      in detail in the second volume of this very good official history.

520   Read, H. *The Annals of Innocence and Experience*. London: Faber and Faber,
      1946; orig. *The Innocent Eye*. 1940. Read, a critic and poet, provides a good
      account of fighting with the 21st Division.

521   Recouly, Raymond. *Foch: The Winner of the War*. Translated by Mary
      Cadwalader Jones. London: T. Fisher Unwin, 1920; orig. 1919. Reasonable
      factual account with some details about the French involvement but not
      analytical.

522   Reichsarchiv. *Schlachten des Weltkriegs: Somme--Nord 1*. [Battles of the
      World War: Somme--North 1.] Band 20. Berlin: Oldenburg, Stalling, 1927.
      Very detailed account of the German defense from July 1 to 13. Argues that
      although the British were inadequately trained, they were very brave and the
      Germans were hurt more than their foes.

523 Reichsarchiv. *Schlachten des Weltkriegs: Somme--Nord 2.* [Battles of the World War: Somme--North 2.] Band 21. Berlin: Oldenburg, Stalling, 1927. Describes in detail the German effort at the Somme in the latter half of July. Suggests that although the British had more casualties than the Germans, the latter were the losers.

524 Reichsarchiv. *Der Weltkrieg 1914-1918: Die militärischen Operationen zu Lande.* [The World War 1914-1918: Military Operations on Land.] 14 Vols. Berlin: E.S. Mittler und Sohn, 1925-1944. German official history. Reduced coverage of the last half of the war, defensive regarding Ludendorff and occasionally very opinionated. Superceded by more recent work.

525 Reid, Brian Holden. "'Yet All Shall Be Forgot.'" *History Today* 36 (July 1986): 6-7. Uses Somme as symbol in discussion of attitudes about the two world wars.

526 Regimental Committee. *History of the East Lancashire Regiment in the Great War 1914-1918.* Liverpool: Libbleburg Brothers, 1936. Provides descriptions of several of the regiment's battalions in action at various battles during the Somme campaign.

527 Regimental History Committee. *History of the Dorsetshire Regiment 1914-1919.* Dorchester: Henry Ling, 1933. History done by battalion and includes description of action at Albert, Bethune, and the Ancre.

528 Regimental Officers. *Das Fusilier-Regiment Prinz Heinrich von Preussen (Brandenburgisches) No. 35 im Weltkrieg.* [The 35th Fusilier Regiment of Prince Heinrich of Prussia (Brandenburgers).] Berlin: Kolk, 1930. Unit served at the Somme in late August and early September. This volume was prepared because the official history of the regiment was regarded as inadequate.

529 Renouvin, Pierre. *La Crise Européenne et la Première Guerre Mondiale.* [The European Crisis and the First World War.] 4th ed. Paris: Presses Universitaires de France, 1962. Although, like many French scholars, Renouvin gives the Somme limited attention, the quality of his scholarship makes his book significant for any study of World War I.

530 Repington, Charles à Court. *The First World War, 1914-1918.* 2 Vols. London: Constable, 1920. Repington was Times' correspondent and his "history" gives day by day account of his experiences. July 6 invited to visit Somme and got to Amiens where he talked to some generals. This is really a discussion of his activities including what he learned about the battle--important mostly in that he had influence in political circles.

531 Reymann, Martin R. *Das Infanterie-regiment von Alvensleben (6 Branden-burgische) Nr. 52 im Weltkriege 1914-1918.* [The 52nd Alvensleben Infantry Regiment (6th Brandenburgers).] Berlin: Oldenburg, Stalling, 1926. History of regiment heavily involved in bitter struggle at Longueval.

532 Richards, Frank. *Old Soldiers Never Die.* London: Faber and Faber, 1933; rpt. 1966 and 1983. Unusually good memoir by soldier in the ranks of the signal corps. His time at the Somme was mostly around High Wood.

533 Richter, Donald. *Chemical Soldiers: British Gas Warfare in World War I.* Lawrence, KS: University of Kansas Press, 1992. Richter provides an excellent scholarly study of the Special Brigade, which was responsible for development and use of gas and other special weapons for Britain. British gas efforts at Loos in 1915 had been more harm than help, and so at the Somme tactical commanders released it well before the actual attack. It had little effect. More useful were the Brigade's new projectors which threw canisters of gas into enemy positions. Also introduced at the Somme was a massive flamethrower that in the end proved too cumbersome to be of much value.

534 Riddell, E., and M.C. Clayton. *The Cambridgeshires 1914-1919.* Cambridge: Bowes and Bowes, 1934. This unit was first involved near Thiepval in early September. It fought in that area until mid-October with heavy casualties but helping in successful attack on the Schwaben Redoubt. The account is descriptive but reasonably detailed.

535 Rifleman A [Smith, Aubrey.] *Four Years on the Western Front.* London: Odham's Press, 1922. The author is unusual in having served for four full years of the war. His account is vivid and articulate.

536 Ritter, A. *Das K.B. 18, Infanterie Regiment Prinz Ludwig Ferdinand.* [The 18th Royal Bavarian Infantry Regiment: Prince Ludwig Ferdinand's.] Munich: Bayerisches Kriegsarchiv, 1926. This regiment of Bavarians was heavily involved in the fighting around Ginchy, Delville Wood, and High Wood during September. Ritter provides a worthwhile account of the German defensive effort and the effect of the British attack on German soldiers.

537 Ritter, Hans. *Der Luftkrieg.* [The Air War.] Leipzig: K.F. Koehler, 1926. Ritter provides a balanced account of the air war and has a good grasp of the emerging strategy of using air power. Air superiority proved a valuable asset to the Entente forces at the Somme.

538 Robertson, William. *Soldiers and Statesmen, 1914-1918.* 2 Vols. London: Cassell, 1926. Robertson, Head of the Imperial General Staff, cites need to relieve Verdun, attrition, and desire to hold German forces in the West as

reasons for the Somme. August 1 he told the Cabinet that these things were happening in hopes of calming concerns about the "butcher's bills." He was much involved in the efforts to ensure Allied cooperation.

539 Robinson, H.[arry] Perry. *The Turning Point: The Battle of the Somme.* London: Heinemann, 1917. Author was a war correspondent, and his book is based on his dispatches. He notes problems and failures but remains upbeat about the effort, quality of soldiers, etc. Overall victory is pretty much assumed. Sounds a bit like P.R.

540 Rockwell, Paul A. *American Fighters in the French Foreign Legion 1914-1918.* Boston: Houghton Mifflin, 1930. Foreign legion units entered the fight on July 3 near Belloy where they had hard fighting. They also fought in August, again with heavy casualties.

541 Rogers, H.C.B. *Tanks in Battle.* London: Seeley Service and Co., 1965. Rogers provides a detailed discussion of the development and early use of tanks. He is very positive about tanks at the Somme, passing lightly over mechanical difficulties and claiming the Germans were terrified.

542 Rogerson, Sidney. *Twelve Days.* London: Arthur Baker, 1933. Although it deals with only the very last of the Somme fighting, this book is an excellent account of the normal condition of a unit in combat.

543 Roskill, Stephen. *Hankey Man of Secrets.* 3 Vols. London: Collins, 1970-74. Hankey was secretary to the Committee of Imperial Defense and privy to considerable inside information. Roskill provides valuable insight into the military/political bureaucracy but only limited comment about the Somme.

544 Ross, Robert B. *The Fifty-First in France.* London: Hodder and Stoughton, 1918. Ross has provided an episodic account of the Gordon Highlanders (51st Division), more valuable for descriptions of living conditions than combat.

545 Ross-of-Bladensburg, John. *The Coldstream Guards 1914-1918.* 2 Vols. with separate vol. of maps. Oxford: Oxford University Press, 1928. The Guards were involved attack in the Ginchy-Les Boeufs Road area on September 15. Expected tanks failed to appear, but the paths planned for them were not shelled, leaving the Guards exposed to flanking machine gun fire. Despite valiant effort attack failed because flank was not secured by equal advances. Unit remained in combat till October 1, losing in its three weeks on the Somme 7,303 casualties. The author notes that tanks which reached battle were considered a brilliant success and quotes Haig's assessment of the battle as his conclusion.

546 Rowlands, D.H. *For the Duration: The Story of the Thirteenth Battalion the Rifle Brigade*. London: Simpkin Marshall, 1932. Descriptive account of the Battalion, which entered the line on July 6 south of La Boiselle opposite Contalmaison and Pozières and July 10th attacked, losing 20 officers and 380 other ranks before being told the attack had been cancelled. In November the Battalion fought at the battle of the Ancre, successfully attacking Beaucourt Trench.

547 Roy, Reginald H., ed. *The Journal of Private Fraser, 1914-1918: The Canadian Expeditionary Force*. Victoria, B.C.: Sono Nis Press, 1985. Fraser was with the Canadians who attempted to take Courcelette on September 15. He was an unusually good diarist with an eye for interesting details about life in the trenches, equipment, and combat.

548 Rule, E.J. *Jacka's Mob*. Sydney: Angus and Robertson, 1933. These memoirs concern the 14th Australian Infantry Battalion in Gallipoli and France and provide a good description of the unit's activities.

549 Rupprecht, Crown Prince of Bavaria. *Mein Kriegstagebuch*. [My War Diary.] 3 Vols. Munich: Deutscher, National Verlag, 1929. Prince Rupprecht replaced Gallwitz as Army Group Commander at the Somme in late August. His assessment of the battle was that if losses like those the Germans had sustained continued they would be forced surrender.

550 Russell, Arthur. *Machine Gunner*. Kineton, Warwickshire: Roundwood Press, 1977. Effective--often quoted--account of the author's experiences, especially at High Wood.

551 Russell, R.O. *The History of the 11th (Lewisham) Battalion the Queen's Own Royal West Kent Regiment*. London: Lewisham Newspaper Co., 1934. The Battalion was not involved until the attack of September 15, but was the unit noted for being in Flers with tanks. This account is particularly valuable because of the involvement of the tanks.

552 Russenholt, E.S. *Six Thousand Canadian Men: Being the History of the 44th Battalion, Canadian Infantry, 1914-1919*. Winnipeg: De Montfort Press, 1932. Russenholt provides a description of 44th in action during the Somme, particularly at Courcelette in September.

553 Samuels, Martin. *Doctrine and Dogma: German and British Infantry Tactics in the First World War*. Westport: Greenwood Press, 1992. More focused on the Germans than the British and with a tendency to give the former too much credit. Samuels does, however, make a useful contribution to the debate over tactics.

554 Sandilands, H.R. *The 23rd Division 1914-1919*. Edinburgh: William Black-wood and Sons, 1925. Clear and effective account of the Division's efforts to take to take Horseshoe Trench and Contalmaison in coordination with the 17th Division. The initial attack, on July 5, was delayed and failed under heavy enfilade fire, but with a renewed effort on July 10th, Contalmaison finally fell. The Division was relieved until July 21 when it returned to the same area for "nibbling" efforts. Later in September the Division fought at Martinpuich and Le Sars.

555 Sandilands, J.W. and MacLeod, N. *The History of the 7th Battalion Queen's Own Cameron Highlanders*. Stirling: Eneas MacKay, Murray Place, 1922. Sandilands served with this unit and might have given a personal view of its attack on Contalmaison in mid-August. Unfortunately his account here is brief and narrow.

556 Sassoon, Siegfried. *Diaries, 1915-18*. Edited by Rupert Hart-Davis. London: Faber and Faber, 1983. Sassoon entered the war in idealistic fashion and became embittered. His diaries show the change and include the often told story of his rescue of a dying man at Mametz during the Somme offensive.

557 Sassoon, Siegfried. *Memoirs of an Infantry Officer*. London: Faber and Faber, 1930; rpt. 1965. Sassoon's fictional account of the war is powerful and bitter, in this volume of his fictionalized autobiography. He was actually involved at the Somme, including being with the 7th Division around Mametz.

558 Schaidler, O. *Das K.B. 7 Infanterie Regiment Prinz Leopold*. [The 7th Royal Bavarian (Prince Leopold's) Regiment.] Munich: Bayerisches Kriegsarchiv, 1922. Schaidler provides a solid unit history with a good account of the German defense against the September 15th attack by the British.

559 Schnitler, Gudmund. *Der Weltkrieg, 1914-1918*. [The World War, 1914-1918.] Berlin: Verlag für Kulturpolitik, 1926. Unusually accurate account of the war. Schnitler suggests that although there was no significant tactical or strategic virtue to the Somme, its effect on morale was very important. The Allies gained confidence while the Germans lost irreplaceable veterans and were shaken.

560 Schoenfeld, Ernst von. *Das Grenadier-Regiment Prinz Karl von Preussen (2 Brandenburgishes) Nr. 12*. [The 12th Grenadier Prince Karl of Prussia's Regiment (The 2nd Brandenburgers).] Oldenburg: Stalling, 1926. Unit heavily engaged in the defense of Longueval during its service at the Somme.

561 Schwarte, Max, ed. *Der deutsche Landkrieg*. [The German Land War.] 3 Vols. Leipzig: Barth, 1921-25. A coherent but incomplete account of the war, and

overly dependent on Haig's dispatches for information about the Somme.

562   Scott, Arthur B., ed. *History of the 12th (Eastern) Division in the Great War,
1914-1918*. London: Nisbet and Co., 1923. Scott has compiled a good
description of the 12th's involvement in the initial phase of the offensive. It
fought with heavy casualties near Ovillers on July 2-7, and then cooperated
with Australian forces in fighting around Pozières in the latter half of the
month. It also fought at Gueudecourt in October. The Division's casualties
for 43 days at the Somme were 10,914.

563   Scott, Frederick George. *The Great War As I Saw It*. Toronto: F.D. Goodchild,
1922; 2nd ed., 1934. Canadian chaplain's account from behind the Canadian
lines near Pozières in September--includes a useful account of caring for the
wounded.

564   Scott, S.J.L. *Sixty Squadron R.A.F.: A History*. London: Heinemann, 1920; rpt.
1990. Scott gives an excellent account of air battles over the Somme but does
not discuss observation for the artillery.

565   Shakespear, J. *The Thirty-Fourth Division 1915-1919*. London: H.F. and G.
Witherby, 1921. Shakespear has written a very readable account of the 34th
Division's bloody attack at La Boisselle, July 1. Although some isolated
groups reached German trenches, the attack failed. The Division remained
in the area, near Pozières, until August 15 when its participation in the
offensive ended.

566   Shakespear, Lt. Col. A *Record of the 17th and 32nd Service Battalions Northumberland Fusiliers (N.E.R.) Pioneers: 1914-1919*. Edited by H. Shenton
Cole. Newcastle upon Tyne: Northumberland Press, 1926. Provides account
of engineering work behind the lines at the Somme battlefield. Some, especially railroad construction near Thiepval, was done under fire.

567   Sheldon-Williams, Inglis, and Ralf Frederic Lardy. *The Canadian Front in
France and Flanders*. London: A. and C. Black, 1920. The account of
Canadian units at the Somme in this book is descriptive and marred by an
affected style.

568   Shephard, Ernest. *A Sergeant-Major's War: From Hill 60 to the Somme*.
Edited by Bruce Rossor with Richard Holmes. Ramsbury: Crowood Press,
1987. Shephard's diary is a very detailed account of his service with the 1st
Dorsets (32nd Division) including attacking in the first week of July near
Leipzig Redoubt. Unfortunately, a lost volume leaves a gap for the rest of the
period of the offensive.

569 Simpson, C.R., ed. *The History of the Lincolnshire Regiment 1914-1918*. London: Medici Society, 1931. Very brief accounts of battalions involved in many of the battles of the campaign.

570 *Sir Douglas Haig's Great Push: The Battle of the Somme*. London: Hutchinson, 1916. Includes many photographs taken as stills from contemporary films of the battle to illustrate a superficial narrative.

571 Sixsmith, E.K.G. *British Generalship in the Twentieth Century*. London: Arms and Armour, 1970. Although the author does not regard Haig as a brilliant general, he does think that Haig was seeking surprise and the chance to exploit gains, achieving some of the former from the French participation and the geographic focus of the attack. He also believes that Haig would have preferred a brief, intense barrage and light infantry to lead the attack for surprise. He was talked out of such plans by Rawlinson, who did not think the troops were up to it. Since Haig had no better solution to the problem of barbed wire, he agreed to a long barrage to break the German front and the infantry moving slowly forward to consolidate and hold.

572 Sixsmith, E.K.G. *Douglas Haig*. London: Weidenfeld and Nicolson, 1976. This volume is more a description of Haig's military activity and analysis of his ideas about strategy and tactics than biography. Sixsmith asserts that Haig is not a great captain because despite an excellent sense of strategy, he lacked a grasp of the tactical and technical aspects of war on the Western Front.

573 Slowe, Peter, and Richard Woods. *Fields of Death: Battle Scenes of the First World War*. London: Robert Hale, 1986. This anthology of soldiers' recollections, including some of the Somme, has unusually good maps to show where the events described occurred. It is a useful introduction to the battles of the war.

574 Smith, Myron J., Jr. *World War I in the Air: A Bibliography and Chronology*. Metuchen, N.J.: Scarecrow Press, 1977. This excellent bibliography has 2035 entries, but often its index does not tie flyers or their units to the ground battles over which they were in action.

575 Smith, Staniforth. *Australian Campaigns in the Great War: Being a Concise History of the Australian Naval and Military Forces, 1914 to 1918*. Melbourne: Macmillan and Co., 1919. Smith provides a useful description of Australians in action particularly at Pozières and Mouquet Farm in July. He offers little comment or analysis other than to praise Australian heroism.

576 Smyth, John. *Leadership in Battle 1914-1918*. Newton Abbot: David and Charles, 1975. Smyth was a World War I officer, and is writing about

leadership among the rank and file and junior officers. He does comment on Haig's use of social ties and public relations skills to rise in rank, but credits the commander with determination. Concerning the Somme, Smyth argues that Joffre wanted attrition, but Haig wanted to punch through and use the cavalry, with the result being disaster. The causes for failure were: Men overloaded; inadequate bombardment (French did better with more concentrated fire); German defenses too good. The long-term effect, however, made the Somme worth the price.

577   South African Official History. *The Union of South Africa and the Great War.* Pretoria: Government Printing and Stationery Office, 1924. Much of the book is devoted to activities in Africa, but the experiences of the 1st South African Infantry Brigade in France and at the Somme are given adequate attention.

578   Spicer, Lancelot Dykes. *Letters From France, 1915-1918.* London: Robert York, 1979. An officer, lieutenant promoted to captain, during the Somme, Spicer provides an account of the King's Own Yorkshire Light Infantry's struggle to remain functional during the offensive while coping with such problems as integrating replacements and maintaining morale. He notes battles but does not describe the action in detail.

579   Spiess, Theodor. *Minenwerfer im Grosskampf.* [Trench Morars in the Great War.] München: J.S. Lehmanns Verlag, 1933. Spiess has studied the use of mortars and devotes a chapter to their use at the Somme.

580   Stacy, B.V. *The History of the First Battalion, A.I.F., 1914-1919.* Sydney: James G. Lee, 1931. Account of a battalion in the 1st Australian Division which was part of the attack on Pozières.

581   Stake, H. Fritz M. *The Worchestershire Regiment.* Kidderminster: Cheshire and Sons, 1928. Battalions of the regiment fought at a number of the battles during the course of the Somme campaign. This make a cohesive study of the regiment at the Somme difficult.

582   Stamps, T. Dodson and Esposito, Vincent J., eds. *A Short Military History of World War I.* West Point, N.Y.: U.S. Military Academy, 1950. Analysis by American soldiers seeking to learn from the problems of others.

583   Stanley, F.G. *The History of the 89th Brigade.* Liverpool: Daily Post, 1919. This is an account of a brigade in the 30th Division which was heavily engaged in the first two weeks of the Somme offensive.

584   Steel, J.P. *A Memoir of Lieut.-Colonel E.A. Steel, D.S.O., R.H.A., R.F.A.*

London: Simpkin Marshall, 1921. Provides an account of the experiences of an artilleryman badly wounded in September at the Somme while serving with the 16th Division.

585 Steele, Harwood. *The Canadians in France, 1915-1918*. London: Fisher Unwin, 1920. Detailed but uncritical description of Canadians involved in combat, with emphasis on naming individuals. Credits Somme with grinding down the Germans so that in 1918 they did not have the men needed to win.

586 Stegemann, Herman. *Geschichte des Krieges*. [History of the War.] 4 Vols. Stuttgart: Deutsche Verlags Anstalt, 1917-1921. Solid survey history with a long chapter concerning the Somme.

587 Stephen, Adrian Consett. *An Australian in the R.F.A.: Being the Letters and Diary of Adrian Consett Stephen, M.C.* Sydney: W.C. Penfold, 1918. Stephen provides a very clear and detailed account of an artillery battery in action at Gommecourt, Pozières, and Thiepval. He notes the communication problems that made accurate infantry support very difficult.

588 Sterling, J. *The Territorial Divisions, 1914-18*. London: Dent, 1922. A short account of twenty divisions. A worthwhile history, but details are necessarily limited.

589 Stern, Albert G. *Tanks, 1914-1918. The Log Book of a Pioneer*. London: Hodder and Stoughton, 1919. Very positive account of tanks in action by an officer involved in producing them. Some details of design are included.

590 Stewart, H. *The New Zealanders in France, 1916-1919*. Auckland: Whitcombe and Tombs, 1921. The second volume in the Official History of New Zealand's Effort in the Great War. This is a popular series intended as a description of New Zealanders' involvement in the war. No effort is made to be scholarly or analytical.

591 Stewart, J. and Buchan, John. *The Fifteenth (Scottish Division) 1914-1919*. Edinburgh: William Blackwood and Sons, 1926. This account focuses on the third phase of the battle, describing preparatory raids in August particularly on Switch Trench, and then the September 15th attack which took Martinpuich, where tanks proved of little use.

592 Stokesbury, James L. *A Short History of World War I*. New York: William Morrow, 1981. Excellent, even-handed one volume survey of the war. Devotes a chapter to the Somme and Verdun.

593 Straz, Rudolph. *Der Weltkrieg: Ein deutsches volksbuch vom den Welt-*

geschehen 1914 bis 1918. [The World War: A German Popular Account of World Events 1914 to 1918.] Berlin: Verlag Scherl, 1933. Includes a chapter concerning the Somme.

594 Sukhachev, S. "Somma." [The Somme.] *Voenno-Istoricheski Zhurnal* 8 (1966): 120-24. Reviews Anglo-French attack, which the author regards as the turning point in the war.

595 Sutherland, D. *War Diary of the Fifth Seaforth Highlanders.* London: John Lane, 1920. Account of a unit in the 51st Division which fought at High Wood in July and the Ancre in November.

596 Swettenham, John. *Canada and the First World War.* Toronto: Ryerson Press, 1969. The strength of this book is in its numerous photographs. Swettenham provides a brief accompanying text, noting the cost of the Somme but asserting that it was worthwhile.

597 Swinton, Ernest. *Eyewitness.* London: Hodder and Stoughton, 1932. Use of tanks at the Somme was foolish and a surprise to Swinton, a leader in the development of the machines, since Haig and his chief of staff expressed agreement with Swinton's memo opposing use. Even if the secret had not been kept, Swinton thinks the Germans would not have had a counter in time. Quotes Ltc. G. Le Q. Martel, *In the Wake of the Tank,* who argues that little was learned. Swinton argues that the technical improvements of the Mark IV could have been made with more testing and the tactics used in 1916 were so bad that they offered little opportunity for meaningful learning.

598 Tames, Richard. *The First Day of the Somme.* London: Dryad, 1990. Pamphlet in the Day That Made History series.

599 Tawney, R.H. *The Attack and Other Papers.* London: Unwin Brothers, 1953. "The Attack," Tawney's brief memoir of attacking and being wounded at the Somme was originally in the *Westminster Gazette* and is also in Vain Glory.

600 Taylor, A.J.P. *English History, 1914-1945.* New York: Oxford University Press, 1965. In this excellent survey, a volume in the Oxford History of England, Taylor sets the Somme offensive in the context of British history and argues that the offensive destroyed a generation of Britons and their idealism as well.

601 Taylor, A.J.P. *Illustrated History of the First World War.* London: Hamish Hamilton, 1963. One of the leading historians of the 20th century, Taylor argues in the traditional mode that the Somme was the "Graveyard of the flower of British manhood," and gained nothing to justify the loss.

602   Taylor, F.W., and T.A. Cusack. *Nulli Secundus A History of the Second Battalion, A.I.F., 1914-1919*. Sydney: New Century Press, 1942. Provides account of a battalion in the 1st Australian Division which was engaged at Pozières in July.

603   Terraine, John. *Douglas Haig: The Educated Soldier*. London: Hutchinson, 1963. Terraine insists that Haig was the very model of a soldier: intelligent, well-trained, in tune with the technology and tactics of his day. He also insists that the Somme, which must be regarded as part of a campaign of several years, was a victory in the sense that it was an enormous drain on the Germans, setting them up for ultimate defeat. He defends the decision to use tanks on grounds of using what was available, and insists that Haig had been planning on using them from the time he first knew they would be available (the numbers promised were much larger than those delivered, of course). Where, Terraine asks, were the critics when the plans were circulated?

604   Terraine, John. *The First World War, 1914-1918*. London: Hutchinson, 1965; rpt. 1983. Well-written short survey laying out Terraine's revisionist view.

605   Terraine, John, ed. *General Jack's Diary 1914-1918*. London: Eyre and Spottiswoode, 1964. Jack was a captain with the 2nd Cameronians in the 8th Division in 1916. He was convinced that the new troops badly needed training and critical of the frequent labor details that interfered with infantry preparation.

606   Terraine, John. "Haig: 1861-1928." *Journal of the Royal United Service Institution* 106 (1961): 491-496. Explores question of Haig's fitness in light of problems in 1916 and 1917 compared to ultimate victory.

607   Terraine, John. "Lloyd George's Dilemma." *History Today* 11 (May 1961): 350-59; 727-28. The problem of communication between British generals Haig and Robertson led to unnecessary casualties.

608   Terraine, John. "Lloyd George's Expedients." *History Today* 13 (April 1963): 219-29 and (May 1963): 321-30. Part one concerns Lloyd George's efforts to bring end to stalemate of 1916. Part two deals with later period.

609   Terraine, John. "1916: The Year of the Somme." *Army Quarterly and Defense Journal* 116 (Oct. 1986): 441-460. Argues that the Somme was a turning point in favor of the Allies.

610   Terraine, John. *The Smoke and the Fire: Myths and Anti-Myths of War*. London: Sidgwick and Jackson, 1980. The quintessential Westerner, Terraine presents and debunks all of the major criticisms of the Somme,

including generalship, use of tanks, and artillery effectiveness.

611   Terraine, John. "The Texture of the Somme, 1916." *History Today* 26 (Oct. 1976): 559-568. Discussion of British strategy and tactics, especially those of Generals Gough and Rawlinson.

612   Terraine, John. *The Western Front.* London: Hutchinson, 1964. This collection of essays is an argument in favor of Haig and the importance of focusing on the conflict in France.

613   Terraisse, Captain. *Avant l'oubli. Histoire vécue du 355e R.I., 1914-1918.* [Before We Forget: Living History of the 355th Infantry Regiment, 1914-1918.] Nice: Bosco, 1964. Account of unit that spent most of the fall of 1916 at the Somme.

614   Thevenet, Général. *La Grande Guerre, 1914-1918.* [The Great War.] Paris: Armand Colin, 1924. Effective account from the French point-of-view. Credits the British effort at the Somme with drawing German forces away from Verdun and allowing successful counter-attacks.

615   Thomas, A. *A Life of One's Own.* London: Gollancz, 1968; rpt.1975. Personal account of experience at the Somme with the 12th Division.

616   Thomas, W. Beach. *With the British on the Somme.* London: Methuen, 1917. Eyewitness account of the entire campaign taken, in part, from dispatches to the Daily Mail.

617   Thompson, Robert. *The Royal Flying Corps.* London: Hamish Hamilton, 1968. Air observation for the artillery and prevention of German observation were vital elements in the British effort at the Somme, and Thompson provides a narrative of the R.F.C. effort.

618   Thomson, P.D. *The Gordon Highlanders.* Devonport: Swiss and Co., 1920; 2nd ed. 1933. Readable unit history with good account of the action at Beaumont Hamel.

619   Thornton, L.H., and Pamela Frazer. *The Congreves.* London: John Murray 1930. Biographies of Walter and William Congreve, father and son, who respectively were general with the XIII Corps and company officer with the Rifle Brigade at the Somme, where the son was killed.

620   Thoumin, Richard. *The First World War.* Edited and translated by Martin Kieffer. London: Martin Secker and Warburg, 1963. First published as *La Grande Guerre.* 3 Vols. Paris: René Julliard, 1960. This book is extracts

from original but published sources. The American edition reduces the space given to the poilu and adds some material concerning English speaking solders. The account of the Somme in American edition is limited.

621 Tilsley, W.V. *Other Ranks*. London: Cobden-Sanderson, 1931. Although fiction, Tilsley's account of a battalion of the 55th Division at the Somme and Ypres gives a good picture of the common soldier's attitudes. His disdain for officers is, however, bitter and deep.

622 *Times* of London, The. *The Times History of the War, 1914-1918*. 22 Vols. London: The Times, 1914-18. Provides a picture of the ongoing knowledge of the conflict in England during the period of the war and helps make clear the level of censorship.

623 Topp, C. Beresford. *The 42nd Battalion, C.E.F.*, Royal Highlanders of Canada in the Great War. Montreal: Gazette Printing Co., 1931. Account of Canadian unit in action in September and October, especially at Courcelette.

624 Travers, Tim. *The Killing Ground: The British Army, the Western Front and the Emergence of Modern Warfare, 1900-1918*. London: Allen and Unwin, 1987. Somewhat revisionist account suggesting that the traditional view of Haig's handling of the battle is too simplistic and that there were a variety of tactical, logistical, and personnel factors that resulted in the failure. Does not, however, exonerate Haig. Regards Haig as "out of his depth" suggesting that he was the product of an outdated "good old boy" system of promotion based in Haig's case on connections at court (this is supported by Clark in *The Donkeys*), and as far as the Somme is concerned thinks Haig was too taken with the idea of a breakthrough, so that he was unprepared for alternatives and lacked a strategic objective.

625 Travers, Tim. "Learning and Decision Making on the Western Front, 1915-1916: The British Example." *Canadian Journal of History* 18 (1983): 87-97. Experience of the Somme and other combat finally forced new tactics and broke the tendency to cling to traditional forms.

626 Travers, Tim. "A Particular Style of Command: Haig and G.H.Q., 1916-18." *Journal of Strategic Studies* 10 (Sept. 1987): 363-76. Haig isolated himself from others and was feared by subordinates, who were reluctant to tell him the truth. He found it difficult to adapt to modern war.

627 Trythall, Anthony J. *'Boney' Fuller: The Intellectual General*. London: Cassell, 1977. Useful biography of leading advocate of tanks with coverage of his service on the headquarters staff of the tank corps in 1916-18.

628   Tucker, John F. *Johnny Get Your Gun: A Personal Narrative of the Somme, Ypres and Arras.* London: William Kimber, 1978. Tucker's memoir is a very detailed account of life and combat as a member of the Kensingtons. He is bitter toward the High Command, which he asserts ordered attacks without visiting the front to observe actual conditions. His description of fighting mostly concerns the Leuze Wood area in the Ginchy-Les Boeufs sector.

629   Turner, John. *British Politics and the Great War: Coalition and Conflict 1915-1918.* New Haven: Yale University Press, 1992. Turner's focus on politics provides little material of importance to the study of tactics and the battlefield, but it is essential context for understanding the pressures on the High Command as it made decisions and planned the Somme offensive.

630   Turner, William. *Pals: The 11th (Service) Battalion (Accrington) the East Lancashire Regiment.* Barnsley: Warncliffe, 1987. Battalion was part of the 94th Brigade, 31st Division, and attacked at Serre on July 1. Casualties were so bad that it was pulled out of the campaign until mid-November. The focus of the book is the July 1 attack.

631   Tyndale-Briscoe, Julian. *Gunner Subaltern: Letters Written by a Young Man to his Father During the Great War.* London: Leo Cooper, 1971. This account includes detailed comments about the technical problems of the artillery such as ranging, coordinating lifts to accommodate the advance of infantry, and communications. The author also describes living and working conditions in the artillery service.

632   Urquhart, H.M. *The History of the 16th Battalion (The Canadian Scottish) Canadian Expeditionary Force in the Great War, 1914-1919.* Toronto: Macmillan, 1932. Thorough account of the unit's activities, including fighting at Pozières, Thiepval, and the Ancre during the Somme. The author is effectively critical of both strategy and tactics employed a the Somme.

633   U.S. Army War College. *German and Austrian Tactical Studies: Translations of Captured German and Austrian Documents and Information Obtained from German and Austrian Prisoners.* Washington: Government Printing Office, 1918. Volume contains two chapters about the Somme, including useful details from the German perspective.

634   U.S. War Office. *History of Two Hundred and Fifty-one Divisions of the German Army which Participated in the War (1914-1918).* Washington, D.C.: War Department, 1920; rpt. 1989. This volume provides an order of battle for the German forces and allows the movement of German units to be traced.

635 Uys, Ian. *Delville Wood*. Rensburg, South Africa: Uys Publishers, 1983. Excellent and detailed history of the South African Brigade's bitter, bloody struggle at Delville Wood, July 14-20. The author has focused on individual soldiers and includes many quotations from personal accounts of the battle.

636 Uys, Ian. *Longueval*. Germiston, South Africa: Uys Publishers, 1983. A short, heavily illustrated book but valuable because it is written from the German perspective and sources. Uys suggests that claims of very high German casualties are well founded.

637 Vale, W.L. *History of the South Staffordshire Regiment*. Aldershot: Gale and Polden, 1969. Vale provides brief descriptions of battalions of the Regiment involved in many of the engagements during the five months of the Somme offensive.

638 Van Creveld, Martin. *Command in War*. Cambridge: Harvard University Press, 1985. Provides interesting comments about the British efforts at command-control during the Somme offensive.

639 Varillon, Pierre. *Joffre*. Paris: Fayard, 1956. This long biography of the French supreme commander provides both background and detail concerning his role in planning the Somme and urging the British to press on at all costs.

640 [Vedette.] *The Adventures of an Ensign: Personal Experience with the Guards on the Somme*. London: William Blackwood and Sons, 1917. Useful memoirs but lacking objectivity and context.

641 Veitch, E. Hardinge. *8th Battalion the Durham Light Infantry 1793-1926*. Durham: J.H. Veitch and Sons, 1927. Most of the book is about World War I and includes accounts of action near High Wood, Martinpuich, and Eaucourt l'Abbaye in September and Butte de Warlencourt in November.

642 Villemont, Emile, and Colonel Domenech de Celles. *Historique de la premiere division de cavalerie, 1914-18.* [History of the First Cavalry Division, 1914-18.] Paris: Dupont, 1924. Cavalry units saw little action on the Western Front, but elements of the 1st Division did serve near Bianches in August and September.

643 Walker, G.A. Cooper. *The Book of the Seventh Service Battalion the Royal Inniskilling Fusiliers from Tipperary to Ypres*. Privately Printed, 1920. Detailed account of the Battalion's activities including fighting at Ginchy during the Somme offensive.

644 Waller, M. Napier. *War Sketches on the Somme Front*. Melbourne: Edward A.

Vidler, n.d. The illustrations taken from sketches done by Waller while serving with the 111th Howitzer Battery, 4th Division, Australian Imperial Forces, give a valuable visual sense of the Somme front. The text provides some context but would not in itself make the book worth consulting.

645   Wanliss, Newton. *The History of the Fourteenth Battalion, A.I.F., Being the Story of the Vicissitudes of an Australian Unit during the Great War.* Melbourne: Arrow, 1929. History of a unit most notably engaged at Fabeck Graben and Mouquet Farm during the Somme.

646   Ward, C.H. Dudley. *The 56th Division (1st London Territorial Division).* London: John Murray, 1921. Ward, an experienced historian, provides a readable account with more contextual information than most unit historians. On July 1 the 56th attack at Gommecourt with initial success, but lack of support resulted in its being driven back by counter-attacks. Its casualties resulted in a move to a quieter area until mid-August. It then returned to the Somme to fight at Ginchy and Flers in September where it found tanks of little help. Wards' conclusion is that the Somme was a success, though the rank and file may not have realized it.

647   Ward, C.H. Dudley. *History of the Welsh Guards.* London: John Murray, 1920. Effective though descriptive account of the unit in action at Delville Wood and Flers from September through November. The author served with this unit and speaks from firsthand knowledge.

648   Ward, C.H. Dudley. *Regimental Records of the Royal Welsh Fusiliers, 1914-1918.* London: Forster, Groom and Co., 1928. This book is actually the third volume of the Regimental Records. Battalions of the regiment served with a number of divisions in action at the Somme. The author is more effective than most at pulling together accounts of such varied activities.

649   Warner, Philip. *Field Marshal Earl Haig.* London: The Bodley Head, 1991. Warner's approach to Haig is mildly positive. He does not try to disguise his subject's faults, but regards many of the problems at the Somme as unavoidable. He argues that the offensive weakened the Germans in ways that could not have been done in any other way.

650   Wauchope, A.G. *A History of the Black Watch (Royal Highlanders) in the Great War, 1914-1918.* 3 Vols. London: Medici Society, 1925-26. This very effective history is broken down by battalions and each volume contains accounts of units active in the Somme campaign.

651   Weiland, Ernst. *Hölle Ginchy.* [Hell at Ginchy.] Eisleben: Winkler, 1930. Extraordinarily vivid account of battle by a Bavarian poet who served with the

7th Bavarian Infantry Regiment at the Somme in September, 1916.

652 Wellmann, Lt. Gen. *Mit der 18 Reserve Division in Frankreich 24 Februar 1915 bis 4 Oktober 1916.* [With the 18th Reserve Division in France 24 February to 4 October 1916.] Hamburg: Rembruber und Henning, 1929. Wellmann's division was assigned to retake Pozières in August and failed, suffering serious casualties in the effort. His account, in diary form, is an interesting description of the battle from the German side.

653 Werner, Johnnes. *Boelcke. Der mensch, der Flieger, der Führer der deutsch in Jagdfliegrei.* Leipzig: K.F. Köhler, 1932. Translated by Claud W. Sykes as *Boelcke: The Man, the Flyer, the Leader.* London: Hamilton, 1933; rpt. 1972. Boelcke was a German air ace, and returned to action in September at the same time as the new Albatross fighter was introduced. Anglo-French airmen, who had enjoyed dominance over the Somme, were put to a much greater test that fall.

654 Westlake, Ray. *Kitchener's Army.* Tunbridge Wells: Nutshell Publishing, 1989. A listing and description of the New Army by division. Information about the offensive is quite limited but the book is useful for identifying which battalions of various divisions were involved in the various battles.

655 Westmann, Stephen K. *Surgeon in the Kaiser's Army.* London: William Kimber 1968. Contains description of German efforts to handle casualties during the Somme offensive. Notes that the bombardment was so fierce "even the rats fled."

656 Weygand, Maxime. *Foch.* Paris: Flammarion, 1947. This short biography of the French commander at the Somme provides some limited comment about Foch's ideas and actions in the campaign. Since the author was also a French World War I general he has an unusual perspective.

657 Whalley-Kelly, H. *"Ich Dien" The Prince of Wales' Volunteers (South Lancashire) 1914-1934.* Aldershot: Gale and Polden, 1935. Battalions of the regiment were at a number of the major battles during the Somme campaign from July to November. Accounts in the volume are brief but offer details not otherwise accessible.

658 White, A.S. *A Bibliography of Regimental Histories of the British Army.* London: Society for Army Historical Research in Conjunction with the Army Museum's Ogilby Trust, 1965. Although it is thorough, the lack of annotations makes this bibliography difficult to use, for entries even include recruiting brochures. It is, however, a very useful reference for finding works about any particular unit.

659   White, Thomas A. *The History of the Thirteenth Battalion, A.I.F.* Sydney: Tyrrells, 1924. Brief history of a battalion in the 4th Brigade most heavily engaged at Fabeck Graben and Mouquet Farm.

660   Whitehorne, A.C., and Thomas O. Marden. *The History of the Welsh Regiment.* Cardiff: Western Mail and Echo, Ltd., 1932. Units of the regiment were involved in a number of the major battles of the campaign. Authors' efforts to follow each battalion make the account cursory at times. Marden commanded a brigade at Mametz Wood, and book has an eyewitness account of that battle.

661   Whitehouse, Arch. *Tanks: The Story of their Battles and the Men Who Drove Them from their First Use in World War I to Korea.* Garden City, N.Y.: Doubleday, 1960. Whitehouse devotes a chapter to the Somme. He thinks that the German High Command expected tanks but failed to tell the rank and file, resulting in some panic. Tank proved that, with a few refinements, it could be formidable weapon.

662   Whitton, F.E. *History of the 40th Division.* Aldershot: Gale and Polden, 1926. Division served at the Somme and was part of the follow up operation after the Germans withdrew to the Hindenburg Line in the winter.

663   Willcox, Walter T. *The 3rd (King's Own) Hussars in the Great War.* London: John Murray, 1925. As a cavalry unit the 3rd did not see action but was repeatedly put in place to exploit a breakthrough. Provides picture of the situation behind the battle lines and is suggestive of the fact that Haig really was thinking breakthrough.

664   William, Crown Prince. *Meine Erinnerungen aus Deutschlands Heldenkampf.* Berlin: E.S. Mittler und Sohn, 1922. Translated as *My War Experiences.* London: Hurst and Blackett, 1922. Crown Prince William was commanding armies at Verdun, but he discusses the effects of the Somme on his situation and the calls for release of men and artillery for use there.

665   Williams, H.R. *The Gallant Company: An Australian Soldier's Story of 1915-1918.* Sydney: Angus and Robertson, 1933. The author began as a sergeant and won a commission. He gives a good account of his service in various units, but only reached the Somme in Oct., 1916.

666   Williams, Jeffrey. *Byng of Vimy: General and Governor General.* London: Leo Cooper, 1983. Williams provides both a description of the Canadian corps, which Byng commanded, in action and some analysis of the overall situation. Canadian divisions moved to the Somme for the September 15th attack on Flers-Courcelette. Byng was not pleased about the rate of casualties

his units suffered (24,019 total at the Somme), but learned about the importance of flexible tactics and limited objectives. This became apparent from the Canadian success at Vimy Ridge the next year. Concerning the overall situation, Williams argues that the point of the Somme offensive was attrition and English horror about casualties was due to lack of experience of the scale of continental war. This is a solid, well-written biography.

667   Williams, M.J. "Thirty Per Cent: A Study in Casualty Statistics." *Royal United Service Institute Journal* 190 (Feb. 1964): 51-55. Williams disputes the assertion in the Official History that thirty per cent should be added to German casualty reports to make up for the failure to report the lightly wounded.

668   Williams, M.J. "The Treatment of the German Losses on the Somme in the British Official History *Military Operations in France and Belgium 1916* Volume II." *Royal United Services Institute Journal* 111 (Feb. 1966): 69-74. Criticizes the procedures used in the official history to determine German casualties and suggests that British losses were "far higher" than German.

669   Williams-Ellis, Clough and A. *The Tank Corps.* New York: George H. Doran Co., 1919. The authors devote a chapter to the first battles in which tanks were used. They suggest problems arose because training conditions were not like the Somme battlefield. These authors think the press was friendly if overly exuberant. The provide a good basic description but little general comment.

670   Williamson, Henry. *The Golden Virgin.* London: Macdonald, 1957. William-son's novel provides a sense of conditions and attitudes during the Somme.

671   Williamson, Henry. *In Spite of All Rejoicing: A Soldier's Diary of the Great War.* New York: Duffield and Co., 1930. Author was at the Somme, and includes some first hand observation of the situation.

672   Williamson, Henry. *The Wet Flanders Plain.* London: Faber and Faber, 1929. The author of this novel was among the attackers at Ovillers and provides a vivid description of offensive action.

673   Wilson, G. Murray, ed. *Fighting Tanks.* London: Seeley, Service and Co., 1929. Written by various soldiers. The general chapter about the Somme is very sparse but a chapter by J.L. Cottle is a personal account of a successful tanker who fought at the Somme.

674   Wilson, Trevor. *The Myriad Faces of War: Britain and the Great War, 1914-18.* Oxford: Polity Press, 1986. The most complete study of British involvement in World War I. Wilson believes that the battle harmed the

Germans more than the Allies, but Haig's success was by luck rather than skill.

675   Wilson, Trevor and Robin Prior. "Summing up the Somme." *History Today* 41 (Nov. 1991): 37-43. The authors argue that although the Somme did contribute significantly to the eventual Allied victory, Haig continued it after conditions were no longer favorable.

676   Winter, Denis. *Death's Men: Soldiers of the Great War*. London: Allen Lane, 1978. Winter disparages British battle training, which he says was not effective until 1917. Even then it emphasized elements that were out of date in the Boer War: leapfrogging lines providing one another covering fire until close enough for a bayonet charge. After the Somme a warning about ignoring cost was removed from the manual but the tactics remained. Men were too heavily loaded also. Most of this book is about the life of the soldier, but enough examples from the Somme to make it appropriate for study of that battle.

677   Winter, Denis. *Haig's Command: A Reassessment*. New York: Viking, 1991. Based on newly available records, Winter rejects a variety of previously accepted views of the Somme. He asserts that the location was not due to French pressure, but was intended originally as a feint for a major strike closer to Ypres. The French, who, despite the common belief that they restricted their effort due to the demands at Verdun, put about the same number of divisions into the struggle as the British and with much more success. Only after the initial engagement did Haig agree with the French pressure for continuing. Unfortunately, British artillery doctrine and skill were hopelessly old fashioned, lacking not only counter-battery techniques and night firing ability, but also the sort of accuracy that would allow shelling the German front line for fear of hitting their own lines. Of course a rolling barrage such as the French used was completely impossible. Furthermore the road and rail network was completely inadequate. Having planned for the major effort to be much further north, Haig did not have more than half the men and guns he said would be needed for a major effort, and the logistical effort could not adequately supply even that level. Haig's original plan was beyond his army's capacity, and the last minute shift to focus at the Somme little short of insanity. He should have refused to continue after the first day.

678   Wise, S.F. *Canadian Airmen and the First World War, Vol. 1, The Official History of the Royal Canadian Airforce*. Toronto: University of Toronto Press, 1980. Provides an account of the use of air power at the Somme with a particular focus on the interrelation of the air and land battles.

679   Witkop, Philipp, ed. *German Students' War Letters*, Translated by A.F. Wedd. London: Methuen, 1929. The letters in this volume represent a cross-section

of educated soldiers. Comments about the Somme are limited but are useful. For instance, Friedrich Steinbrecher, a veteran of the Eastern front and soon to die, wrote in late August about how the English with the help of the R.F.C. were blasting German batteries.

680 Wolinski, Jean-Jacques. *La Vie d'une division. La 18e D.I., Mémoire de Maîtrise.* [The Life of a Division. The 18th Infantry Division, Memories of Mastery.] Paris: Sorbonne, 1968. The 18th Division only arrived at the Somme in October, but its history provides a picture of the conditions and combat of the latter part of the offensive.

681 Woodward, David R. *Lloyd George and the Generals.* East Brunswick: Associated Universities Press, 1983. In-depth analysis of Lloyd George's involvement with the military, providing important background to the political elements in strategic planning.

682 Woolnough, F. G. *A Short History of the Royal Tank Corps.* Aldershot: Gale and Polden, 1925; 2nd ed., 1931. Author notes bad ground and inadequate training contributed significantly to the failure of tanks at the Somme. Only 32 of 49 tanks got to starting points on September 15. There were individual successes but generally not much success. The machine's potential for the future was shown, however.

683 Worthington, Larry. *Amid the Guns Below: The Story of the Canadian Corps.* Toronto: McClelland and Stewart, 1965. Worthington provides a brief survey of the Canadian divisions' participation in the offensive. Although he praises Julian Byng, the English general who commanded the Canadians, he is very critical of Haig and the overall plan. He asserts that the battle was a strategic miscalculation and marked by tactical errors. The sacrifice in casualties was not justified.

684 Wren, Eric. *Randwick to Hargicourt: History of the 3rd Battalion, A.I.F.* Sydney: Ronald G. McDonald, 1935. History of a battalion in the 1st Australian Division which was part of the attack on Pozières in July.

685 Wright, P.L. *The First Buckinghamshire Battalion, 1914-18.* London: Hazel Watson and Viney, 1920. This Battalion was part of the 48th Division, which was engaged at Albert, Bazentin Ridge, and Ovillers in July, Pozières Ridge in August, and the Ancre in November.

686 Wylly, H.C. *The 1st and 2nd Battalions The Sherwood Foresters (Nottingham and Derbyshire Regiment) in the Great War.* Aldershot: Gale and Polden, 1926. The First Battalion was battered at the Battle of Albert. The second was committed in the September-October fighting at Flers-Courcelette,

Morval, and Transloy. This is a thorough though almost entirely descriptive account of the actions.

687 Wylly, H.C. *The Green Howards in the Great War.* Richmond, Yorkshire: [Butler and Tanner], 1926. Provides accounts of the regiment's battalions which served independently at a number of the battles in the Somme campaign.

688 Wylly, H.C. *History of the 1st and 2nd Battalions the Leicestershire Regiment in the Great War.* Aldershot: Gale and Polden, [1928.] These units were mostly involved in mid-September at the Quadrilateral near Ginchy and Leuze Wood. Although they had tanks, the machines were of little help. Coverage in the book is descriptive.

689 Wylly, H.C., ed. *History of the King's Own Yorkshire Light Infantry.* 3 Vols. London: Percy Lund, Humphries, n.d. Battalions were in action at the beginning of the campaign at Thiepval Wood and Ovillers and later at a number of other battles. Accounts include useful details but are quite brief. Volume 3 concerns World War I and is by R.C. Bond.

690 Wylly, H.C. *History of the Queen's Royal Regiment.* Vol. 7. Aldershot: Gale and Polden, n.d. Accounts follow battalions which were scattered during the campaign. Coverage too brief for much value except as details of particular units.

691 Wynne, G.C. *If Germany Attacks: The Battle in Depth in the West.* London: Faber and Faber, 1940; rpt. 1976. Wynne provides interesting descriptions and comments on the German defensive tactics on the Western Front, including the Somme campaign.

692 Wyrall, Everard. *The Die-Hards in the Great War: A History of the Duke of Cambridge's Own (Middlesex Regiment), 1914-1919.* 2 Vols. London: Harrison and Sons, 1926-30. Six battalions of the regiment were in the first attack and in following their efforts on July 1 and in later action the coverage becomes quite fragmented.

693 Wyrall, Everard. *The East Yorkshire Regiment in the Great War 1914-1918.* London: Harrison and Sons, 1928. The unit was at many of the major battles between July and November, but the account is choppy due to the author's effort to follow each battalion. Context is reasonable, and an account of tanks in combat is included.

694 Wyrall, Everard. *The Gloucestershire Regiment in the Great War, 1914-1918.* London: Methuen, 1931. Effective accounts of the regiment in action at

Bazentin Ridge, Pozières and High Wood in July and September. Casualties were very heavy.

695 Wyrall, Everard. *The History of the Duke of Cornwall's Light Infantry 1914-1919*. London: Methuen, 1932. Unit was at the Somme from July 14 until mid- November fighting at High Wood, Delville Wood, Guillemont, Flers- Courcelette, Le Transloy, and the Ancre. The author who wrote a number of unit histories does a competent job of describing its activities.

696 Wyrall, Everard. *The History of the Fiftieth Division 1914-1919*. London: Percy Lund, Humphries and Co., 1939. On September 7 the 50th took over the sector north and northeast of Bazentin-le-Petit where it suffered badly September 15-22. It fought effectively at Flers-Courcelette suffering heavy casualties. The author claims much credit for taking High Wood, all of which had previously gone to the 47th Division. At the Battle of Morval, 25-28 September, the 50th helped take Combles, Les Boeufs, and Gueudecourt. Division also fought at Transloy on October, 1-18, and Gird Trench and Hook Sap November, 13-19. All of this action involved a gain of about 3.5 miles. Wyrall provides his usual competent description.

697 Wyrall, Everard. *The History of the King's Regiment (Liverpool) 1914-1919*. 3 Vols. London: Edward Arnold, 1928-35. Traces the activities of the regiment's battalions in detail, at key points day by day. Volume two (1930) includes accounts of many of the significant battles of the Somme campaign.

698 Wyrall, Everard. *The History of the 19th Division 1914-1918*. London: Edward Arnold, 1932. July 1 the 19th was to attack La Boisselle, from which the enemy could enfilade the attack front. The village was stoutly held, but the 34th and 8th Divisions on the flanks were suffering and so the attack had to be pressed. By evening of July 2nd the village was occupied, but the next morning counter-attacks began. July 6 the Division was relieved. Brigades from the 19th fought again July 29th at Pozières and High Wood and at the Battle of the Ancre, November 13-18. Wyrall, though he sticks very closely to official records, does a good job of describing the action.

699 Wyrall, Everard. *The History of the Second Division 1914-1918*. 2 Vols. London: Thomas Nelson and Sons, 1922. Elements of the Division were in action at Delville Wood, Guillemont, and Beaumont Hamel. Wyrall provides a workmanlike descriptive account of the fighting.

700 Wyrall, Everard. *The History of the Somerset Light Infantry (Prince Albert's) 1914-1919*. London: Methuen, 1927. The author has done numerous unit histories and gives reasonable account of the Somme, following the unit's various battalions in action from July through November.

701   Wyrall, Everard. *The 17th (S.) Battalion Royal Fusiliers 1914-1919*. London: Methuen and Co., 1930. This Battalion was not committed to the Somme campaign until late July but then fought for three months with little result except heavy casualties. Major actions at Guillemont, Delville Wood, and the Ancre. Book provides competent coverage of the situations.

702   Wyrall, Everard. *The West Yorkshire Regiment in the Great War 1914-1918*. 2 Vols. London: John Lane, The Bodley Head, Ltd., 1924-27. The section about the Somme is more than 100 pages and provides a detailed account of most of the major actions from July through November.

703   Young, A.J., and D.W. Warne. *Sixty Squadron, Royal Flying Corps*. Singapore: Eurasia Press, 1967. The authors provide an account of the R.F.C. squadron's efforts in 1916 that were central to the Anglo-French air superiority over the Somme.

704   Zwehl, H. von. *Erich von Falkenhayn*. Berlin: E.S. Mittler und Sohn, 1926. This biography is brief but well done, and is useful for its picture of the German command's reactions to the opening of the Somme offensive.

Index

Numbers shown in regular type refer to entry numbers in the annotated bibliography. Numbers in bold type refer to pages in the opening essay. Numerals have been treated as if they were spelled out.

About the Compiler

FRED R. VAN HARTESVELDT is Professor of History at Fort Valley State College in Georgia. He is editor of the anthology, *The 1918–1919 Pandemic of Influenza* (1992), and the author of a number of reviews and articles.

www.ingramcontent.com/pod-product-compliance
Lightning Source LLC
Chambersburg PA
CBHW060349100426
42812CB00003B/1179